wa............
and began his car.................................gn. Since
1978 he has work.........ance writer and consultant in the
field of architectural history and the history of the decorative
arts. His publications include *By Hammer and Hand: The Arts
and Crafts Movement in Birmingham* (editor and contributor,
1984) and *C. R. Ashbee: Architect, Designer and Romantic
Socialist* (1985), which won the Duff Cooper Memorial Prize
and the Henry-Russell Hitchcock Award. His research for
Charles Rennie Mackintosh was supported by the South Square
Fellowship of the Royal College of Art
in London

WORLD OF ART

This famous series
provides the widest available
range of illustrated books on art in all its aspects.
If you would like to receive a complete list
of titles in print please write to:
THAMES AND HUDSON
30 Bloomsbury Street, London WC1B 3QP
In the United States please write to:
THAMES AND HUDSON INC.
500 Fifth Avenue, New York, New York 10110

Printed in Singapore

Alan Crawford

CHARLES RENNIE MACKINTOSH

167 illustrations, 25 in color

Thames and Hudson

For Sarah and Kate

1 (*frontispiece*) Glasgow School of Art. Centerpiece of the north front, 1896–99.

© *1995 Thames and Hudson Ltd, London*

First published in the United States of America in 1995 by Thames and Hudson Inc., 500 Fifth Avenue, New York, New York 10110

Library of Congress Catalog Card Number 94–62072
ISBN 0–500–20283–4

Printed and bound in Singapore

Contents

778889

Acknowledgments

I am grateful to the Royal College of Art, whose award of the South Square Fellowship in 1992–93 enabled me to do the research for this book in Glasgow.

Much of the research was done in the Hunterian Art Gallery of the University of Glasgow. I am grateful to all the staff there for their help and kindness, and especially to Pamela Robertson who has care of the Mackintosh material. This book owes a great deal to her helpfulness and enthusiasm, and to her habit of strewing inconvenient facts in my path.

I am grateful to Liam Southwood and Bronwen Thomas for the care they have taken with the plans and sections which illustrate the book. And I would like to thank the owners of buildings designed by Mackintosh who have shown me round, and the staff of the Charles Rennie Mackintosh Society, Glasgow School of Art, The Hill House, the Mitchell Library, Glasgow, the Planning Department of Glasgow Corporation, Scotland Street School Museum, Strathclyde Regional Archives and the archives of the University of Strathclyde.

For help of various kinds I thank Louise Annand, Roger Billcliffe, Annette Carruthers, Jerry Cinamon, Patricia Douglas, Graham Dry, Anne Ellis, Zsuzsanna Gonda, Murray Grigor, Susie Harries, Janice Helland, Melissa Johnson, Wendy Kaplan, Juliet Kinchin, Pat Kirkham, James Macaulay, Billy Mann and the staff of the Western Baths, Colin and Valerie Miller, Alistair Moffat, Karen Moon, Michael Moss, Stefan Muthesius, Matt Neilson, Eva B. Ottillinger, Iain Paterson, George Rawson, Daniel Robbins, Philip Rodney, Nicolas Rüsch, Sally Rush, Andrew Saint, Gavin Stamp, Mrs Donald Taffner, David Walker and Toshio Watanabe.

It has been a pleasure for me to witness, at Thames and Hudson, the care, sensitivity and sheer speed with which a book can be published.

Lastly, I am especially grateful to Perilla Kinchin, who read the final draft of this book and improved it greatly, in matters of fact and nuances of meaning.

For illustrations, acknowledgment is due to: T. & R. Annan & Sons 13, 31, 36, 47, 50, 52, 54–56, 57, 70, 95, 115, 122, 132, 133, 164 – Cassina s.p.a. 165 – Christie's Images 8 – Alan Crawford 11, 19, 26, 29, 33, 35, 37, 45, 51, 87–90, 102, 105, 161, 166 – In Edinburgh: The National Trust for Scotland 107, 108, 112, 128; Royal Commission on the Ancient and Historical Monuments of Scotland 3, 34, 44, 101, 103, 104, 110, 111, 136, 138; The Trustees of the National Library of Scotland 81; © Trustees of the National Museums of Scotland 30 – Photo Keith Gibson 1 – In Glasgow: © The Glasgow Picture Library 99; Collection: Glasgow School of Art 14, 17, 23–25, 27, 43, 71, 116, 129, 134, 135, 137, 141, 149, 150, 160; © Hunterian Art Gallery, University of Glasgow, Mackintosh Collection, Glasgow (Photo Media Services, Glasgow University) 15, 16, 18, 20, 21, 38–42, 49, 58, 60–65, 67, 69, 72–76, 78–80, 83–85, 92, 94, 96–98, 106, 109, 113, 114, 120, 121, 124, 126, 127, 139, 142, 145, 148, 152–156, 158, (Photo Anne Dick) 125, (Photo Antonia Reeve) 143; The Mitchell Library, Glasgow City Council 6, 9 – Japan Art & Culture Association, Tokyo 167 – In London: © The Trustees of the British Museum 157, 159; Courtesy of the Board of Trustees of the V & A 66, 119, 146 – The Manchester Public Libraries, Central Library 91, – Private Collection 82, 144 – Private Collection, Photo courtesy Roger Billcliffe 151, 162, 163 – © Photo R.M.N. 118 – Photo Douglas Scott 140 – Photo Edwin Smith 2 – The Royal Commission on the Historical Monuments of England, Swindon 5, 28. Plans and sections, except ill. 155, © Liam Southwood and Bronwen Thomas

Foreword

In this book I have told the story of Mackintosh's life and work, and in doing so I have come across three problems.

The first is that we do not know a great deal about his life. Many drawings survive to document his work, but for his personal life there are relatively few letters, two brief diaries, some lecture notes, and scattered and sometimes contradictory reminiscences. Admirers of Mackintosh are given to speculating about him; the lack of evidence seems to encourage them. But I would ask the reader to respect the gaps in our knowledge, and to recognize that, for much of Mackintosh's life, we simply do not know what he thought or felt.

The second is that certain episodes in Mackintosh's career have been distorted by earlier writers. They have argued that his talents were only appreciated by a few enlightened patrons in his native Glasgow; that his work was rejected by the English at an early stage in his career; that it was acclaimed in Vienna in 1900 and thereafter enjoyed a major reputation in Europe; and that, as a result of being welcomed abroad and cold-shouldered at home, Mackintosh decided, in about 1914, to leave Glasgow for good. This story has its roots in the writings of Hermann Muthesius during Mackintosh's lifetime. After Mackintosh's death it became canonical, because it suited the history of Modernism in architecture and design. And it has survived the demise of Modernism because it also fits the Romantic stereotype of the lonely artist-hero. In a book as short as this I have tried to avoid debates with other writers. But this distorted version of Mackintosh's career is so widespread that I have had to take account of it. I have called it the Mackintosh myth and, at appropriate points, given a different version of events. In order to substantiate the myth, I have generally quoted from the standard work, *Charles Rennie Mackintosh and the Modern Movement* by Thomas Howarth, first published in 1952. But I should emphasize that the myth did not start with Howarth's book and extends far beyond it. (A fuller account of the myth is given in Chapter Seven.)

The third problem is that, at the height of his career, Mackintosh worked in an informal collaboration with Margaret Macdonald, whom he married in 1900. His most expressive interiors belong to this phase, and in 1927 he wrote to Margaret that she was half, if not three-quarters of the inspiration for his architectural work.[1] The essence of their collaboration was not that he did some things and she did others – though sometimes that was the case – but that many interiors which are usually attributed to him seem to be permeated with her influence. In the middle of this book, therefore, I have written that 'the Mackintoshes designed' this or that, where I would otherwise have written 'Mackintosh'. This joint attribution works well enough for the central collaborative works, such as the interior at 120 Mains Street, Glasgow, or the Rose Boudoir exhibited in Turin; but with others, including the interior of The Hill House, I have felt its clumsiness and inconsistency.

A note on spelling

Mackintosh was born Charles Rennie McIntosh, but changed the spelling of his name to Mackintosh in the early 1890s. I have adopted the usual spelling throughout, but have referred to his family as McIntosh. Conversely, Herbert McNair is often spelt MacNair, but as he only used this spelling for a few years round 1900, I have adopted McNair.

CHAPTER ONE

Growing up in Glasgow
Firpark Terrace 1868–1891

Charles Rennie Mackintosh was born on 7 June 1868 at 70 Parson Street, in the oldest part of Glasgow. His father, William McIntosh, was a policeman, an upright man and strict in his observation of the Sabbath; his only unPresbyterian virtue was a passion for gardening, and the McIntoshes' flat was always full of flowers. Mackintosh's mother, born Margaret Rennie, is remembered as a woman of character, warm-hearted, and much loved by her family. In twenty-three years of marriage she gave birth to eleven children, of whom Charles was the fourth.

The McIntoshes belonged to the upper echelon of the working class. William McIntosh had a steady, respectable job and, perhaps, an instinct for bettering himself. No. 70 Parson Street was a tenement, a block of flats such as most Glaswegians lived in, but the McIntoshes' flat had three 'windowed' rooms, according to the census returns, when two-thirds of Glaswegians lived in one or two. By modern standards, life was crowded, but Charles Rennie Mackintosh did not grow up in a slum. In tenements, most of the principal rooms had beds in them, and a large family could sleep in a few rooms with dignity. When Charles was six, the family moved to 2 Firpark Terrace, a new tenement in the suburb of Dennistoun which aspired to be middle-class; there they had five windowed rooms. It was only a short distance away, but it was a step up. For Mackintosh, growing up in a Glasgow tenement did not mean poverty or disorder. But it did mean living closely with parents, brothers and sisters. And it meant learning about death: three of his sisters and one brother died in infancy. Afterwards, presumably, the orderly houseproud family life closed around them.

At the age of seven he went to Reid's Public School, and at nine to Allan Glen's School in Cathedral Street, a private school for the children of tradesmen and artisans which specialized in practical subjects. We do not know how he got on. The playground probably had its terrors for him, for he was not strong and was born with a contracted sinew in one foot which made him limp as he grew older. And in the classroom he suffered from some kind of dyslexia. He had difficulty with spelling for many years, as passages quoted later in this book will show. Architecture attracted him at an early age, perhaps as an alternative to both the playground and the classroom. On the way home from school each day he would pass the Necropolis, Glasgow's spectacular hillside Victorian cemetery. It was a perfect place for boys to play, testing each other's daring among the mysterious, overstated monuments, hiding in the porches of mausolea. What did Mackintosh, perhaps doubtful in play, make of this strange landscape, these child-size houses with no one in them?

In 1884, at sixteen, he started work as a pupil in the office of John Hutchison, a little-known architect, at 107 St Vincent Street. Walking westwards each day across the city, Mackintosh would trace a path through its history: past the great Cathedral, almost the only relic of medieval Glasgow; across the top of what is now called the Merchant City, where traders built up Glasgow's fortunes as a port in the 17th and 18th centuries; and then over Buchanan Street into the commercial centre of the city. Here a grid of handsome residential streets had been laid out in the early 19th century, on Glasgow's small but sudden hills. At that time, Glasgow's wealth had come, like Manchester's, from cotton. But by 1884 grand banks and offices, telling of even greater prosperity, were spreading westwards, displacing the quiet town houses. Now the sources of wealth included the mining of coal and iron-ore in Lanarkshire, heavy engineering, chemicals and, above all, ship-building. Between 1870 and 1913 Clydeside shipbuilders consistently provided a third of the total British tonnage.

Power in the city lay with the merchants and the churchmen, for Presbyterianism penetrated middle-class life in Victorian Scotland to an extent now difficult to recapture, and it was exercised most obviously through the progressive policies of the City Corporation. On his way to work, Mackintosh would have watched the slow building of the Corporation's massive City Chambers in George Square, and noted perhaps the sumptuousness of its interiors. We have got used to the idea that art could have a strong and independent life in the big, industrial cities of late Victorian Britain, and it flourished nowhere more vigorously than in late Victorian Glasgow. An imaginary frieze representing 'Art in Glasgow' would include Alexander Reid, dealer in international art and friend of Van Gogh; William Burrell, shipping magnate and collector of medieval decorative art, Oriental ceramics and Impressionist paintings; Alexander Thomson, architect of parochial scope and international stature; and the group of open-air

2 The Necropolis, looking south-east over the spires and chimneystacks of Glasgow. The gable end of Firpark Terrace, where Mackintosh grew up, is on the extreme left of the picture.

painters known as 'The Glasgow Boys', whose broad handling of light and colour, influenced by France, Holland and Japan, was beginning to enjoy a reputation in Europe. Indeed, Glasgow felt itself to be a European city. In size and structure it was like Birmingham, Liverpool or Manchester. But it was also the largest city in Scotland, whose history and identity were not English.

While working for Hutchison, Mackintosh attended classes at Glasgow School of Art. In the late 19th century, young men learned to be architects in the office where they worked, but the talented or ambitious also went to art classes. There Mackintosh would sit in front of a group of cubes and cones, or a cast of historic ornament, working in a precise and unexpressive way, acquiring general drawing skills. He worked hard, winning prizes in examinations, threading his way through the intricate syllabus of the National Course of Instruction which was devised by the Department of Science and Art in London and shaped the teaching in most British art schools.

In 1885 the Governors of Glasgow School of Art appointed a young and vigorous Headmaster, Francis Newbery, whose attitudes fostered the young Mackintosh's early career. Newbery understood Glasgow's vitality in the arts. But he also wanted the School to succeed in the eyes of the Department of Science and Art. He cared about the decorative arts and the nascent Arts and Crafts movement. And, most importantly for Mackintosh, he cared about individual creativity. From the start, Mackintosh attended architecture classes, and his earliest independent works were speculative designs made for competitions such as the Department of Science and Art's mammoth annual National Competition. 'A public hall' is a later and more skilful example of these designs. They are highly finished, but heavy with the weight of teaching and a young man's ambition. The quick, loose style of drawing he used on sketching trips from the late 1880s, though humble and as yet undistinctive, held more promise.

In December 1885 his mother died. He was seventeen.

On the completion of his pupilage in 1889, Mackintosh joined the firm of Honeyman and Keppie, which consisted of two principals and three or four draughtsmen, with offices at 140 Bath Street. John Honeyman was fifty-eight, a courteous man of wide and scholarly interests, with a distinguished record of buildings. But his practice had suffered a disastrous drop in income in the second half of the 1880s, and when he took John Keppie as a partner in 1888, it was perhaps a rescue operation. Keppie was only twenty-seven, but he was the son of a wealthy Glasgow merchant, and brought new capital and clients to the practice. He came with excellent credentials: he had trained with James Sellars, the last of Glasgow's distinguished Classicists, and had then studied in Paris, where ambitious young Glaswegian architects liked to go, and won prizes in competitions. Though wealth, class, sophistication and the hierarchy of the office separated Mackintosh from Keppie, Mackintosh was only six years younger, and his talents complemented Keppie's. In the newly constituted firm, Honeyman seems to have been a reassuring presence in the background; Keppie was said to be good at running the practice, but was only a competent designer. So there was an opening, indeed a need, for a talented designer. During the first half of the 1890s at least, the principal works of Honeyman and Keppie were probably the work of Keppie and Mackintosh.

The practice belonged to Glasgow's architectural élite. Both partners had been or would be presidents of the Glasgow Institute of Architects, and Fellows of the Royal Institute of British Architects in

6

London; they had scholarship and good connections. In Honeyman's hands the practice had been the fourth in Glasgow in terms of value of work handled, and would be again in Keppie's. But that work was not particularly specialized or glamorous; architects in big industrial cities probably did not turn many jobs away. A little under half of it was work on houses, less than a quarter on churches, and the rest comprised shops, offices, industrial buildings and schools in roughly equal quantities. New buildings made up only one fifth of the total. The rest was alterations and additions, a porch added here, a new roof for a church hall there.

The architecture of 19th-century Glasgow was marvellously coherent. It was almost entirely built of stone, a buff sandstone at first and then, from about 1890, a deep plum-red sandstone from quarries in Ayrshire and Dumfriesshire. And it was by tradition a Classical city, like its rival Edinburgh. In most British cities around the 1850s the pressure of city-centre redevelopment, shifts in taste, and new building types and materials toppled Classicism from its pre-eminence. But in Glasgow Classicism remained, stretched to breaking point,

3 Robert Rowand Anderson: Central Hotel, Gordon and Hope Streets, Glasgow, 1879–84.

fragmented, but still there, in Italianate buildings which answered the need for a richer architectural language, in the treatment of iron façades, and above all in the extraordinary work of Alexander Thomson, who invested the warehouses, tenements, churches and villas of Glasgow with monumental forms that are variously Greek, Egyptian and wholly abstract.

Thomson died in 1875, and it has been said that the Classical tradition in Glasgow almost died with him. In the 1880s and 1890s, when Mackintosh was beginning his career, Glasgow's architecture became more plural and various. Two buildings of the 1880s illustrate the new directions. The Central Hotel is of 1879–84 and was designed by the Edinburgh architect Rowand Anderson. It combines a generalized Scottishness with freedom and variety (loose grouping, a picturesque skyline and an eclectic range of sources). This combination, new to Glasgow, would characterize its progressive architecture in the 1890s.

The Athenaeum was designed by the Glasgow architect J. J. Burnet in 1886. The style was Classical as befits an Athenaeum, but for Burnet style was not the point. He had studied at the École des Beaux-Arts in Paris, and became the principal British exponent of its disciplined, rational approach, which grounded the whole design of a building in a clear plan and a firm grasp of practical essentials. For Burnet, style was simply a matter of appropriate dress, and the elevation was required to be a clear expression of the plan. (It is easy to assume that the free style of the Central Hotel offered a clearer expression of the plan than the Classical style of the Athenaeum. But the assumption is false.) Burnet was the rising star of Glasgow architecture in the 1880s, and Mackintosh admired him. Round 1900 he was

4 John James Burnet: the Athenaeum, 8 Nelson Mandela Place, Glasgow, 1886. From *The Builder*, 9 July 1898.

5 John Belcher: Institute of Chartered Accountants' building, Great Swan Alley, off Moorgate, London, 1888–93.

the city's most distinguished architect, charming, honoured in Britain and abroad, and immensely skilful. His rational Classicism would be at the forefront of British architecture in the 1900s. Thus his presence is woven, like a commentary, through much of Mackintosh's career.

Though Glasgow's architectural life was vigorous and independent, it was not shut off. The nine-and-a-half-hours' journey to London was easily done overnight by train. And Glasgow architects read the English building papers, for there was almost no local architectural journalism. They would have felt the Gothic and Classical allegiances of the mid-century softening, in the 1870s and 1880s, into a lighter, more eclectic mood. A refined, and often inventive, Gothic continued to be used for church work, but for public and commercial buildings, progressive architects turned to German and Flemish Renaissance, English brick architecture of the time of Wren, and even latterly the Baroque. (Witness the plastic, sculptural façades of the enormously influential Institute of Chartered Accountants' building 5

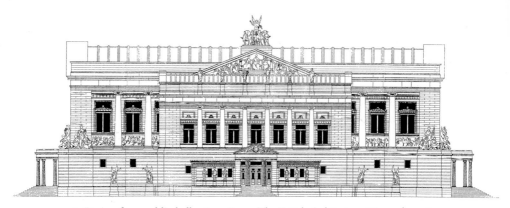

6 Design for a public hall, 1890. From *The British Architect*, 21 November 1890.

of 1888–93.) For houses in the suburbs or the country, English farm-houses and small manor houses of the 16th to 18th centuries, altered and added to over the years with picturesque awkwardness, offered a suitable model, rural and essentially English. English architecture must always seem soft and various to Scottish eyes; but never so much as at this time, with its pretty red brick pediments, its bands of terracotta ornament, its tile-hanging and timber-framing.

These late Victorian styles were given separate, sometimes fanciful, names – Gothic, Old English, 'Queen Anne'. But it is more appropriate here to call them by one of the names which were used at the time, the Free Style. To the leaders in these developments – Richard Norman Shaw, John Belcher, Philip Webb, J. D. Sedding – eclecticism was a vehicle of freedom, a real and practical kind of modernity. In Scotland the Baronial style, which drew its inspiration from Scottish castles and tower-houses of the 16th and 17th centuries, expressed similar aspirations, but with a stronger nationalist charge.

In 1890 Mackintosh entered the competition for a Travelling Studentship in memory of Alexander Thomson with a thoroughly Greek design for 'A public hall'; the winner would receive £60 towards a three-month sketching tour. He won, and decided to go to Italy; if more money had been forthcoming, he would also have gone to the south of France. On 10 February 1891, five weeks before he set out, he gave a lecture to the Glasgow Architectural Association on 'Scotch Baronial Architecture' which showed that his sympathies did not lie, in the end, with Classicism. Scottish Baronial, he argued, was Scotland's national architecture. You could learn to love the works of

Greece and Rome, but they were foreign in spirit and far away. In his lecture notes we read: 'How different is the study of Scottish Baronial Arch. Its original examples are at our own doors . . . the monuments of our own forefathers the works of men bearing our own name . . .'[1]

But while Mackintosh believed in Scottish Baronial, he had an eye on other things. He presented the tradition as developing through four phases, and 'rejoicing in the full attainment' of its objects in the fourth, from about 1550 to about 1650, when the upper stages of tower-houses were elaborately corbelled and turreted above plain walls, more for the sake of decoration than protection.[2] (All this was taken directly from the first three volumes of *The Castellated and Domestic Architecture of Scotland* by David MacGibbon and Thomas Ross, then in course of publication.) His taste was at odds with his ideas here, for any of the earlier, more austere periods would have served his nationalist argument better. He preferred the time when Scottish tower-houses were becoming less stern and more domestic, the time when English influences were felt. He preferred it because, in that fourth phase, they grew to be sophisticated, flexible and ornamental, qualities which were precisely those of the Free Style.

On 21 March 1891 Mackintosh left Glasgow. He had not been outside Britain, and perhaps not outside Scotland, before. In Naples he filled his days with churches and museums, sketching when he

7 Crathes Castle, Kincardineshire. From David MacGibbon and Thomas Ross, *The Castellated and Domestic Architecture of Scotland*, vol. 2 (Edinburgh 1887).

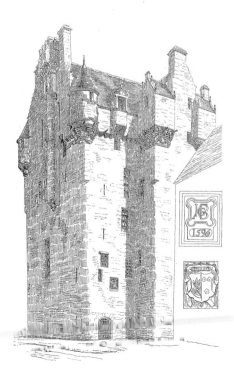

could and writing up his diary in the evening. The poverty and idleness appalled him; 'beggerly Italians', he wrote, 'loafing blackguards'.[3] He was young and in a strange land. From Naples he went to Sicily and wondered at the mosaics at Monreale. Throughout the tour he was mainly drawn to Early Christian, medieval and early Renaissance work, and to detail and decoration more than plan, structure or mass. Then he went north through Rome and the glorious towns of Umbria and Tuscany. Florence was full of good things, but he responded blandly, as if handing out marks: 'S. Lorenzo. Medici Pew, good. Library. benches and windows very good. Cloister poor.'[4]

8 Ravenna and Venice were high points too, but by June he was beginning to tire, and at Cremona had to force himself to sketch; at the beginning of July he came home. He had seen much that he admired, and, for a year or two, plundered his sketchbooks when working on competition designs. But Italy did not have much influence on his work. Crossing the Alps into Italy was, for many northern European architects at this time, an experience that changed their lives and their work. Mackintosh had perhaps gone too soon.

8 Sketch of a well head in Venice, 6 June 1891. Pencil.

CHAPTER TWO

Architect and Artist
Regent Park Square 1891–1900

Mackintosh came home from Italy in the summer of 1891, to the tenement in Firpark Terrace where he had grown up. But in the following year his family moved to a terrace house in Regent Park Square, a very respectable street south of the Clyde. William McIntosh had been promoted to Superintendent in 1889, and could afford something more than a tenement flat. And perhaps he needed to, for on 8 July 1892, he married Christina Forrest, a widow from Dennistoun. About a year later they moved again, but then came back, around Christmas 1895, to a house at 27 Regent Park Square. The young architect was not close to his father after the second marriage; but, so far as we know, he lived in the family home throughout the 1890s, and was idolized by his little sisters. At 27 Regent Park Square he had a room in the basement, which he decorated with Japanese and Pre-Raphaelite prints, and a stencilled frieze of his own designing.

His Italian tour would have increased his standing in the office of Honeyman and Keppie, and in this chapter we shall follow the development of his architectural talents to a point of real maturity. But there are two other, subsidiary themes. One is art. He began to think of himself as an artist, counted artists as his closest friends, and took up the decorative arts. The other is reputation. Mackintosh was ambitious, perhaps as much for what he believed in as for himself. And during the 1890s the machinery of reputation (exhibitions, reviews, articles in magazines) played an increasingly important part in his career.

For about eighteen months his work as a draughtsman at Honeyman and Keppie included no new buildings. But the competition designs which he did in his own time and the lectures he gave helped to make his name known. 'Clever' is what *The British Architect* called his chapter house of 1891 in an Italian Renaissance style, and his railway terminus of 1892, both unsuccessful bids for the Soane Medallion of the Royal Institute of British Architects; 'clever' too was their assessment of Honeyman and Keppie's final entry in the impor-

9 Detail from a design for Glasgow Art Galleries, 1891–92. From *The British Architect*, 8 July 1892.

9   tant Glasgow Art Galleries competition.[1] Critics in the 1890s often used this word of Mackintosh's work, and I have used it in this book. The critics used it in a two-edged way, implying admiration for Mackintosh's work and a suspicion that it was a young man's work, facile, merely fashionable. I have used it to suggest a facility in Mackintosh's work which actually deepened with time, a sense of design which, while it depended crucially on cleverness and the handling of surface forms, grew to be far from superficial.

The competition designs were academic in character, but they show his tastes developing. They were enriched with panels of scrolling foliage and the little cartouches that Renaissance putti hold (as were his decorations for the Glasgow Art Club's new premises of 1892). These are the beginnings of his interest in line and imagery. Equally, the lectures were clumsily expressed and painfully dependent on published writings, but they reveal his allegiances. He lectured twice about his Italian tour, once on 'Elizabethan Architecture', and twice on 'Architecture'. In the second 'Architecture' lecture, delivered in February 1893, he pinned his colours to the mast of the English Free Style: 'I am glad to think that now there are men such as Norman Shaw – John Bentley – John Belcher Mr Bodley Leonard Stokes and the late John D Sedding . . . men who more & more are freeing themselves from correct antiquarian detail . . . We must clothe modern ideas with modern dress – adorn our designs with living fancy.'[2]

In 1893 he got his first big architectural job. The publishers of *The Glasgow Herald*, the city's principal middle-class daily paper, asked Honeyman and Keppie to build at the back of their Buchanan Street premises, in Mitchell Street and Mitchell Lane, at a cost of about £30,000. They wanted a water-tower in case of fire (the scourge of printing offices at this date), and a clear route past the dispatch room for their vans. Otherwise the new building was to be an ordinary warehouse, not specifically designed for printing, and was let as such at first. 10–12

Mackintosh put the tower on the corner, more than 150 feet (some 46 metres) high. The angles of its upper stages are decorated with cartouches (now so elongated that they look like elephants' trunks), and it is crowned with a pretty ogee roof, echoing James Maclaren's tower at Stirling High School (1887–89), and Sedding's on Holy Trinity, Sloane Street, London (1888–90). It was a powerful gesture, but only loosely related to the rest of the building in its upper stages, and perhaps too powerful for the narrow Mitchell Street, over which it broods.

The Mitchell Street front is orderly, with gabled bays at either end, an off-centre staircase bay, strong cornice, and Scots Renaissance dormers contributing to the picturesque skyline. The ornateness of the upper part, as of the tower, recalls Mackintosh's admiration for 17th-century Scottish Baronial. On Mitchell Lane the treatment was simpler.

It is the restless, witty details of the *Glasgow Herald* building that reveal the hand of the young Mackintosh. The first, second and third floors were identical in plan, but Mackintosh designed the windows on each floor differently, and set the bowed and canted glazing back to show the thickness of the wall, as Halsey Ricardo had done in London at 8 Great George Street, Westminster, in 1888. He drew out some of the mouldings in a swagger way, turning strapwork into flickering tongues; others he let die gently into the wall. Others again were vehicles for wit: the second-floor staircase window has a square-

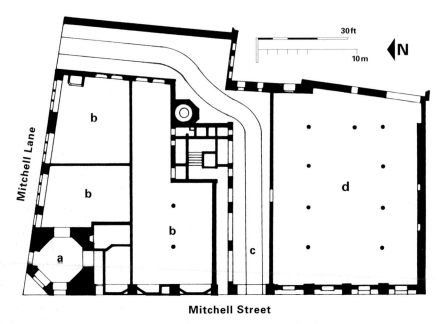

30 ft
10 m
N

Mitchell Lane

b

b

b

a

c

d

Mitchell Street

a entrance hall, **b** warehouse and offices, **c** route for newspaper vans, **d** dispatch room

11 section architrave; the first floor staircase window has the stonework round it recessed in a square section, like a negative architrave; while above each window is a wedge-shaped stone like a keystone, neither projecting nor recessed but floating, so to speak, flush with the wall. In 1900 this building was included in Hermann Muthesius's survey of Free Style architecture in Britain, *Die englische Baukunst der Gegenwart*, where its Scottish plainness and boldness stood out amongst the English work, despite the clever details.

Glasgow Herald building, Mitchell Street and Mitchell Lane, Glasgow, 1893–95

10 Plan of the ground floor.

11 Negative architrave and floating keystone at the first-floor staircase window.

12 Mitchell Street front. From Hermann Muthesius, *Die englische Baukunst der Gegenwart* (Leipzig and Berlin 1900).

13 The architect as artist: Mackintosh photographed by T. & R. Annan in 1893.

13   In 1893 Mackintosh had himself photographed at T. & R. Annan's in Sauchiehall Street. He wore a loose collar and a tie gathered in a big, mock-careless bow, like W. B. Yeats. He presented himself, not as a young provincial architect, not as a professional man, but as an artist. The portrait can stand for his discovery of new images, new friends and a new identity at around this time.

  In these years his best friend was probably Herbert McNair, a draughtsman who had joined Honeyman and Keppie in 1888. They both went to classes at the School of Art in the evening, along with other working men. John Keppie's sister, Jessie, was also a student, but she went during the day, when the students were mostly middle-class women. At about this time there was a romantic attachment between Mackintosh and Jessie, and it may have been through her that he and McNair became part of a group of talented women students who
14 called themselves 'The Immortals'; they included the sisters Margaret and Frances Macdonald. Old photographs show them larking about at Keppie's house in Prestwick. And their curious, hand-made periodical, 'The Magazine', preserves their watercolour paintings and designs.

24

14 The Immortals at play. From left to
right: Frances Macdonald, Agnes Raeburn,
Janet Aitken, Charles Rennie Mackintosh,
Katherine Cameron, Jessie Keppie,
Margaret Macdonald.

15 Margaret Macdonald: *Summer, c.* 1893.
Pencil, pen, ink and watercolour.

The work of the Macdonald sisters was different from the rest. They painted thin, androgynous women, sometimes painfully elongated, standing among stylized lines which may be swirling hair or branches and buds. The pictures were influenced by the verse-dramas of the Belgian poet Maurice Maeterlinck, with their timeless melancholy, and by the Symbolist Movement. But they are not always easy to understand. They leave you with a sense of apartness. Contemporary critics decried the physical distortion, but were, perhaps, more deeply disturbed by their unconforming eroticism and their associations with the 'New Woman'. Feminist art historians have seen in them a bleak protest against the effects of patriarchy. Here we should simply note that, despite the distortions of their style, their subjects were not always sad or sinister. In *Summer*, probably a design for a stained-glass window, the sun-god kisses alive the plants of the earth.

Mackintosh had painted a loosely symbolic watercolour, *The Harvest Moon*, in 1892, McNair a much stronger one, *The Lovers*, in 1893; the work of the Macdonald sisters was already mature. In 1893–94 these four came together as artists, and there began a phase of collaboration which lasted for several years. It is said that they were immediately christened 'The Four', and it is convenient to call them that, though the name actually seems to have been given post-humously. McNair later emphasized the importance of symbolism in their work: 'not a line was drawn without purpose, and rarely was a single motive employed that had not some allegorical meaning.'[3] For Mackintosh this was a moment of great importance, but one whose consequences unfolded gradually.

We know that he was thinking about symbolism at this time, for his 1893 lecture on 'Architecture' drew heavily on *Architecture, Mysticism and Myth* (1891) by W. R. Lethaby, the most thoughtful of contemporary English architects. Lethaby's book was a plea for a symbolic architecture, and was influential, for a time, in the circles of the Free Style architects whom Mackintosh admired. Working with The Four perhaps enlarged his sense of its possibilities. But it was a slow process, and Lethaby's book itself had no immediate influence on his work. He began to use the same images as the Macdonalds – tall, dreaming women, rose trees, suns – but not, perhaps, with their full depth of meaning, as we shall see. The imagery that was to be peculiarly his own, less figural, more organic and perhaps more abstract, took time to develop.

Being one of The Four freed Mackintosh's imagination. And being one of The Immortals freed him socially and personally. When he

16 A sketch of houses in the High Street, Broadway, Hereford and Worcester, *c.* September 1894. Pencil.

stepped across the social divide between evening- and day-classes, when he presented himself as an artist, Mackintosh was both claiming a place in the middle class and holding that class at arm's length. As an example of social mobility, it was subtler and more immediately effective than his father's hard work but not, as it turned out, so enduring. And when he stepped out of the all-male office of Honeyman and Keppie, and into the company of young women artists whose sense of themselves was at odds with patriarchy, he was liberated and inspired, for his imagination was sensitive to femininity, and it flowered in the company of women.

In September 1894 Mackintosh set off on a sketching tour in the north Cotswolds, whose vernacular buildings had recently been extolled in *The Builder*: 'all their charm depends on the honest, simple, and unaffected way in which they are treated.'[4] Throughout his career, Mackintosh's sketchbooks reflected his changing architectural tastes, and in 1894 he was the typical Free Style architect in search of vernacular honesty. He drew church details, 17th-century houses and bits of old furniture, mostly in quick, matter-of-fact freehand elevations. The next four summers were spent like this in England, the sketching style becoming looser and more mannered each year.

16

27

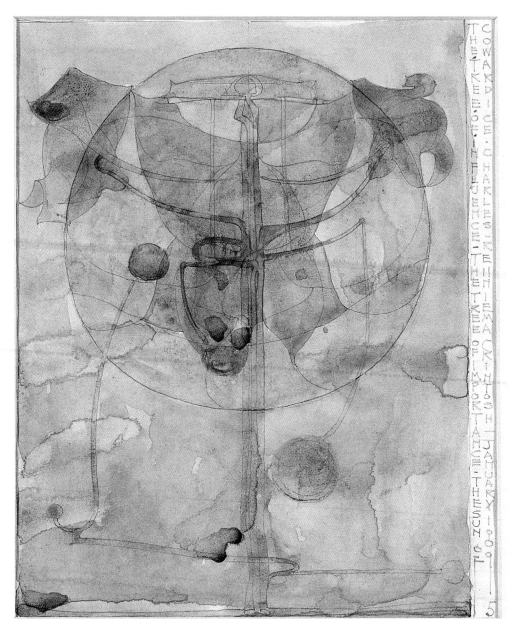

17　*The Tree of Influence. The Tree of Importance. The Sun of Cowardice*, 1895. Pencil and watercolour.

Soon after he got back, work by the Macdonald sisters went on show at the Glasgow School of Art Club exhibition. It is not clear what was exhibited, but it stirred up violent protest and debate. 'Ghoul-like' is what the critics said, 'impossible forms, lurid colour, and symbolism that requires many footnotes of explanation'; though they also said that 'no one who has seen the nightmare work . . . can fail to be impressed by its cleverness'.[5] This was the beginning of the sisters' notoriety, in which Mackintosh and McNair shared. The nickname 'The Spook School' was probably given to them at this time.

In January 1895 Mackintosh painted a pair of symbolic watercolours which later appeared in 'The Magazine'. Their intense, private, structured symbolism is almost unique in his work, and they are of great importance. It is hard to disentangle the meanings of the elaborate titles which are lettered down the sides – what traditional symbolism connects the sun with cowardice? – but both of the images themselves show something like an upright, stylized tree standing in the same plane as a containing circle, suggesting the mutuality of male and female. A tree can be upright, male, upholding. There is a fairly direct line from these watercolours to timber uprights in Mackintosh's buildings.

18 Poster for Glasgow Institute of the Fine Arts, 1895. Colour lithograph.

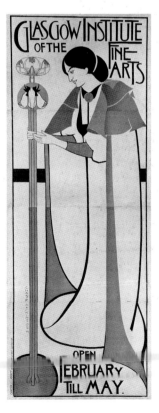

In February the annual exhibition of the Glasgow Institute of the Fine Arts was advertised with a poster by Mackintosh. Like other progressive artists of the 1890s, The Four were keen to adapt their paintings to the relatively new and popular medium of the pictorial poster, and Mackintosh designed several. His designs were less distorted and less visually ambitious than equivalent work by the Macdonalds, but they were in the same mould. The papers said his Glasgow Institute design 'caused the hair of the Philistine to curl'.[6] It showed a cloaked woman grasping a stylized, phallic-looking flower. The style was sufficiently close to Aubrey Beardsley's for the reference to be unmistakable. Thus it worked on several levels. On the surface, it was a typical artistic poster of the 1890s, with the formula of a generalized female figure and a striking graphic style. A little below the surface lay the allusion to Beardsley, which made it an image of the decadent avant-garde, designed to shock. And below that again was the sexual imagery, which might be recognized but could not be publicly admitted. Did it also work as an image of The Four, using their own particular symbolism? That is not clear.

   The next few months, until June 1895, were probably spent on the design of a new Board School: the spread of free and compulsory education in the late 19th century brought a lot of work to architects. In many respects, Martyrs' Public School is conventional, but the roof timbers are not. The trusses over the stairs are pegged in the style of Japanese timber-framing, which Mackintosh may have learnt about from Edward S. Morse's *Japanese Homes and their Surroundings* (1886).

And while the hall rafters seem to rest on paired brackets which read as part of a continuous roof system, perhaps beams projecting from the next-door rooms, the brackets are actually little bits of wood about 18 inches (61 centimetres) long, tacked onto an equally flimsy upright; the continuity is only apparent. Mackintosh was not interested in structural techniques, but he was fascinated by their appearance. Give him timber and he would create a hybrid structure, with some parts doing ordinary mechanical work and others simply seeming to.

19 Martyrs' Public School, 11 Parson Street, Glasgow, 1895–97. Roof of the hall. Removal of plasterwork during repairs has revealed the 'quasi-construction' of the paired brackets.

20, 21 Sideboard, *c.* 1896. Oak, stained dark. The detail shows the mouldings under the bottom drawer.

Mackintosh had in fact been designing in wood for some years. His earliest datable free-standing furniture belongs to 1893, and he showed several pieces at an Arts and Crafts exhibition in Glasgow in April 1895. The twenty or so items which he designed in the mid-1890s were generally cupboards or other carcase furniture, made of oak or cypress; the chairs for which he is famous came later. And they were simple in design and construction, as 'artistic' furniture could acceptably be. Mackintosh's hand was felt, as in his buildings, in the studied, almost eccentric details: the bottom drawer of the sideboard of *c.* 1896 has a swelling front with fascia and cyma recta mouldings **20, 21** tucked right underneath it, perfectly formed but so easily overlooked that Thomas Howarth thought the lower part of the cabinet 'severely plain . . . all unnecessary mouldings are omitted'.[7] Most of these designs were occasional commissions and not, like much of his later work, part of an interior for which he was also responsible.

Early in 1896 Honeyman and Keppie were invited to compete for the design of buildings for Glasgow School of Art. The School flourished under the headmastership of Newbery and the guidance of James Fleming, pottery manufacturer and Chairman of the Governors; but it occupied cramped rooms in Sauchiehall Street when other cities had purpose-built art schools. Early in 1893 Fleming and Newbery inspected the art schools at Birmingham and Manchester, probably

Glasgow's closest rivals. In autumn 1895 a site was acquired in Renfrew Street, facing north but sloping southwards down one of Glasgow's steepest hills, and in June 1896 the Governors issued a competition brief which had considerable influence on the design, since it specified the size of studios, their need for north light, and the height and design of north-facing windows. It was made clear that the building should be plain. In January 1897 Honeyman and Keppie were declared the winners of the competition. It has always been accepted that their design was by Mackintosh. But the Minutes of the Building Committee show that overall responsibility, and decisions taken as the building was going up, fell to Keppie as the partner involved.

22   Mackintosh's plan set out the principal floors as a shallow E resting on a rectangular basement. There was a central core of services, circulation and administration: heating chamber, entrance hall, staircase, Headmaster's room and studio, and the museum, a large toplit space for the display of historical examples and students' work. Almost all the studios were ranged on either side of this along the north front: modelling and architecture in the basement, ornament, still-life and design on the ground floor, and painting from life and the antique in the lofty first-floor studios. Miscellaneous uses such as the library, board room and caretaker's house went in the two outer wings, where the fall of the site allowed a building of five storeys, compared with three on the north front; the difference in height played a vital part in Mackintosh's design. As a result of the Governors' detailed brief, the plan as a whole clearly reflects the requirements of the Department of Science and Art, and bears a family resemblance to that of Manchester School of Art (1878–81).

In the event, the Governors could only afford to build the central and eastern part of the building in the 1890s. When it was completed

22 Glasgow School of Art, 167 Renfrew Street, Glasgow, first phase of building, 1896–99. Plans. The part of the building west (right) of the entrance hall, Headmaster's room and museum was not built.

FIRST FLOOR   **a** life room (male), **b** life room (female), **c** Headmaster's room, **d** advanced antique room, **e** elementary antique room, **f** board room, **g** museum, **h** flower painting
MEZZANINES ABOVE   **i** staff studio (male), **j** staff studio (female), **k** Headmaster's studio (over c)

GROUND FLOOR   **a** lecture theatre, **b** elementary ornament, **c** advanced ornament, **d** office, **e** entrance hall, **f** advanced still-life, **g** elementary still-life, **h** design room, **i** male staff room, **j** female staff room, **k** cloakroom, **l** library
MEZZANINES ABOVE   **m** lunch room, **n** upper part of library

BASEMENT   **a** life modelling, **b** elementary modelling, **c** advanced modelling, **d** heating chamber, **e** coals, **f** students' common room, **g** anatomical study, **h** architectural drawing, **i** building construction, **j** caretaker's house (lower floor), **k** metalwork, **l** packing room, **m** store, **n** china painting, **o** needlework, **p** wood carving, **q** stained glass, **r** lecture theatre
MEZZANINE ABOVE   **s** caretaker's house (upper floor)

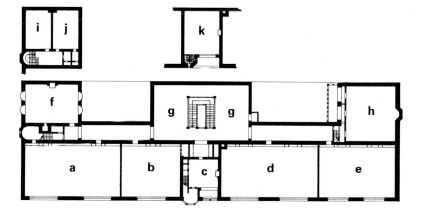

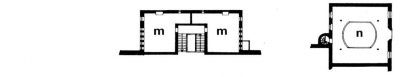

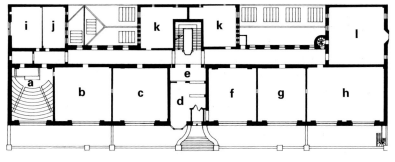

100ft

30m

N

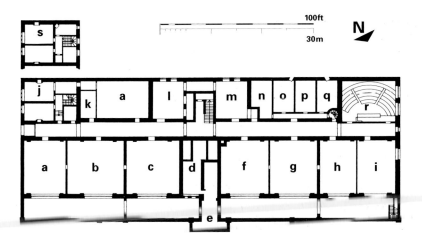

23 Glasgow School of Art. A composite photograph of the north front.

129, 130
23
1
ten years later, the west wing was entirely redesigned and a third floor of studios was added. But the long north front followed the original design. It consists of two elements: a centrepiece, whose entrance is exactly in the middle of the building, and ranges of studios on either side. In front of the centrepiece, steps rise to the entrance between S-curved walls; a two-storey oriel beside the entrance lights a caretaker's cubby hole and, above, the Headmaster's lavatory; the Headmaster's room is over the entrance, with a balcony slicing across the oriel; above that is his studio, set back and reached by a stair tower. The elements of this design are mostly the middle-size, vernacular, domestic features which were the usual vocabulary of Free Style architecture. The oriel and balcony, for instance, were inspired partly by an old house at Lyme Regis in Dorset which Mackintosh sketched in 1895, and partly by James Maclaren's 12 Palace Court, London, of 1889–90.

We can see the centrepiece in two different but familiar ways: as a focus of display, dignifying the centre of the building like a Classical portico, and as the honest expression of the plan, intricate in some places, rugged in others. There is truth in both these points of view, but we will not understand the design until we run them together, and accept that much of the honesty is actually display. There is more going on here than either use or propriety requires: the Headmaster has a never-used balcony (the School of Art enjoys magnificent views,

34

but they are on the other side of the building) and the tower rises
much higher than the stair it encloses. The excitement in the inter-
locking forms of the lower part and in the picturesque massing of the
upper was generated in Mackintosh by the possibilities of composition, not by the necessities of planning. Here, as in so much Free Style
architecture, Invention is the mother of Necessity.

The studios are quite different, calm and austere under their deep
eaves. In Renfrew Street, you cannot take in the whole front in elevation. But elevation drawings and composite photographs reveal
asymmetries and subtle syncopations within the overall design, in the
number of windows on either side, their widths, the intervals between
them and the intervals of the railings at the front. These are, however,
variations on a symmetrical theme. The design is firmly balanced
around the centrepiece, and this effective symmetry is able to embrace
elements of discontinuity in the design. In the street, you take the
symmetry for granted, and are more struck by the bareness of the
studio ranges. The wall is unworked apart from the curved reveals of
the windows and a slight setback level with the lintels; there are no
architraves; and the lintels are left as rolled-iron joists cased in plaster,
as if this was the back of the building. Here Mackintosh gave the
Governors plainness. The austerity of the studios is, if anything,
heightened by the delicate ironwork, especially the brackets with their

24   flower-like knots of intertwined metal; these provide supports for the window-cleaners' planks, and help to brace the glazing bars.

25   The east side of the building was divided roughly in two by one carefully placed down-pipe. The five-storey wing on the left contained the caretaker's house on the two lowest levels, the staff room above that, then the board room, and then top-lit staff studios reached by a stair tower. Unlike the centrepiece on the north front, this wing is loosely composed – you could add to it without disruption. But the choice of features is equally arbitrary: the handsome pediment which dignifies the Headmaster's room on the north front here adorns the male staff room; neither plan nor propriety requires that the board room should have bow windows like an 18th-century shop; and Mackintosh's busy and brilliant forms at the base of the stair tower merely embellish a models' changing room. The area to the right of the down-pipe, on the other hand, the return wall of the studios, was completely blank. (The windows to the right of the door date from 1915.) In relation to the studios, this blankness is a matter of function – there was no reason why Mackintosh should break up the wall with windows; but as part of the entire east side, and in relation to the east wing, it is a matter of composition.

        If we consider the east side as a whole, it is like an open book, with one page filled in and the other not. If we consider the building as a

24 Glasgow School of Art. Wrought-iron brackets at the first-floor windows.

25 Glasgow School of Art. The east front.

whole, the north front as well as the east side, then the blank is at least a pause in the design, such as occurs between the chapters of a book or the verses of a poem. And perhaps, given the difference between the north front and the towering east wing, it is more than this: a break, a place which engenders excitement because the design reads as if it were in danger of collapsing. Here, for the first time, we find a deeper cleverness in Mackintosh's work, a handling of façades that goes beyond composition, into a drama in which the spectator is invited to take part.

1, 26   If we return to the centrepiece in Renfrew Street, we find the main entrance framed by a deep, subtly curved architrave; the mouldings rise into leaf-like forms or merge with the flowing hair and clothes of two women, who kneel in the central medallion with a stylized rose-bush between them. This is more than the graceful simplification of traditional mouldings which Free Style architects practised. There is ambiguity, as wall merges into moulding and moulding into imagery; and there is a symbolic design typical of The Four, framing the entrance to their (new) spiritual home. We are reminded of

8   Mackintosh's symbolic watercolours of 1895, with their juxtaposition

26 Glasgow School of Art. The entrance.

27 Glasgow School of Art. The staircase.

28 Glasgow School of Art. The museum.

of upright and enclosing lines. In the centre of the entrance is a tall wooden post whose spreading cap touches the lintel. This is a tree. Originally the doors which flank it were hung at the back of the porch, so that the upright stood by itself, a boundary-post and playful image of support.

The stairwell beyond the entrance hall is constructed, like the rest 27 of the building, of steel infilled with concrete. But that is not at all what you see. For this is another of Mackintosh's constructional fantasies, where the hidden, horizontal steelwork has left him free to play with overstated vertical timbers. The balusters rise to a horizontal rail running out from the highest step of each flight. At the front, the newel post rises from floor to ceiling, and at the back two newel posts rise from the half-landing in the basement to the balustrade of the museum, an impossible height of more than 30 feet (9 metres). As they reach the level of the museum floor, they are clasped between twin beams in the manner of Japanese house-construction. Mackintosh created a hanging cage of verticality through which you ascend to the light of the museum. There, four posts mark the corners of the stairwell. They also run up to the inner trusses of the roof with spreading caps, but by now we have seen too much to take them seriously as supports. So Mackintosh, the smiling showman, hangs two more caps from the outer trusses, without any posts.

Glasgow School of Art is a young man's design, and reveals its architect's enthusiasms. It has debts to Scottish tower-houses and English vernacular (especially in the centrepiece and east wing). The twin beams of the staircase and the metal discs on the front railings were inspired by Japan. The Headmaster's window and its duplicate on the east side both have the glazing set back behind the mullion, in the manner of Alexander Thomson. And there are many connections with the work of contemporary Free Style architects. Some are Scottish like Maclaren, Burnet (the eaves cornice and architrave of the east entrance) and H. E. Clifford (the bow windows of the board room). Others are English: the curved cornice of the pediment over the Headmaster's window may be compared with the first-floor windows of Belcher's Institute of Chartered Accountants, the boundary wall and railings with those on Smith and Brewer's Passmore Edwards Settlement in Tavistock Place, London (1895–98), and the dipped parapet of the east wing with Voysey's 14–16 Hans Road, London (1891–92), the gable above it with Voysey's 1892 design for 'Studios in a London Street', and the horizontal rails and vertiginous newel posts of the staircase with Voysey's practice generally.[8] Mackintosh probably meant only the references to Scottish tower-houses and English vernacular to be read as allusions.

Glasgow School of Art is a Free Style building. The merging and interpenetrating forms of the centrepiece and east wing make it perhaps the most original in Britain. But it goes much further than any other Free Style building in a particular direction. There are details which leave you wondering about Mackintosh's intentions, like the lowest course of stonework on the two-storey oriel of the centrepiece, which has an abruptly different form from the curved and splayed courses above. Or the Headmaster's pediment, whose segmental curve is not continuous with the horizontal but juts out above it in a tiny but marked discontinuity. And there are larger discontinuities: between the horizontal north front and the vertical east side, as we have seen, between the façadism of the centrepiece and the functionalism of the studio ranges, and between the inside of the building and the outside. Free Style architects designed buildings which,

29 Glasgow School of Art.
Detail of the two-storey oriel.

however loose the composition, however juxtaposed the elements, followed a single programme. Here, it seems, Mackintosh did not. The School of Art is a discontinuous, fractured work, open to many interpretations. Much of its originality consists in that.

It took three and a half years to build the first phase of the School of Art, from the initial design in 1896 to the opening at the end of 1899. For Mackintosh these were years of growing reputation and increasingly varied work. In September 1896 he and the Macdonald sisters sent work to London to be shown by the Arts and Crafts Exhibition Society. This was important, for the Arts and Crafts Exhibitions were the principal showcase for progressive decorative art in Britain. Mackintosh displayed a hall settle, a symbolic watercolour   30 entitled *Part Seen, Imagined Part*, and two beaten brass panels; the Macdonald sisters a clock in beaten metal, and two beaten aluminium panels. According to the Mackintosh myth, these exhibits were greeted with scorn and rejection. Thomas Howarth wrote: 'The unheralded appearance of the work of *The Four* evoked a storm of protest from public and critics alike. . . . The English Arts and Crafts Society . . . stolidly maintained its attitude of scornful derision, and the Scottish designers were not invited again to exhibit south of the border.'[9]

It is hard to substantiate this story from the surviving evidence. The only magazine to pay much attention to Mackintosh and the Macdonalds was *The Studio*. Its reviewer was less interested in reporting the work they exhibited than in reviving the debate which their work had stirred up in Glasgow in 1894–95: ' "the spooky school" is a nickname not wholly unmerited', he wrote; 'No doubt in Glasgow there is a Rosetta stone, which makes clear the tangled meaning of these designs.'[10] He presented Mackintosh and the Macdonalds as new, young and controversial, and added that 'Probably nothing in the gallery has provoked more decided censure than these various exhibits.'[11] But if there was censure, it must have been confined to visitors to the exhibition. Most of the reviews did not mention The Four at all, for they were almost unknown in London, and those that did showed no particular hostility to them. The most established architectural weekly, *The Builder*, illustrated Mackintosh's settle, praising its logical use of decorative construction.[12] It seems that the English did not find the work of Mackintosh and the Macdonalds as disturbingly radical as Howarth supposed; it was the Glaswegians who had made the fuss. As for the Arts and Crafts Exhibition Society, Mackintosh exhibited with them on two subsequent occasions.[13]

31   A few months later Mackintosh was at work on stencil decorations for Miss Cranston, the *doyenne* of 'artistic' tea-room proprietors in Glasgow, who was putting up a new building in fashionable Buchanan Street. Most of the decorations and the furniture were by George Walton, a young but experienced Glasgow designer. But Miss Cranston, hoping perhaps to harness the sense of scandal which had

30 Hall settle, 1895. Oak, stained dark, with beaten lead panels and stencilled linen upholstery.

31 Miss Cranston's Tea Rooms, 91–93 Buchanan Street, Glasgow. The lunch gallery, 1896–97.

greeted The Four in Glasgow, asked Mackintosh to decorate the walls of a general lunch room on the first floor, with a lunch gallery and smoking gallery stacked above it. From the light well you could just see all three levels at once, so Mackintosh used a green ground at the bottom, greyish-greenish-yellow in the middle and blue at the top, giving a sense of lower earth, middle earth and sky. His stiff designs consisted of tree-like forms between peacocks at the bottom; in the middle, tall haloed women enmeshed in rose-bushes, with a tree-like form between them that ended in something like the section of a fruit, or a vulva; and at the top, shapes like totem-poles and a wavy line like clouds running across the face of a sun or moon. Mackintosh had adapted the imagery of The Four to tea-room decoration. This was certainly the weird new art which Miss Cranston wanted as a talking point, and clouds in the smoking gallery were appropriate male whimsy. But the meanings of the women in the lunch gallery, and perhaps other images, were private to The Four; and the phallic and vulva-like character of the 'tree' was publicly inadmissible. Here, as in his poster designs, there was a gap between public, ornamental functions and private, symbolic meanings.

32–35 During the first half of 1897 Mackintosh worked on a new church and church hall at Queen's Cross, in the expanding district of Springbank. For the Free Church of Scotland, he designed a single preaching space with one gallery at the east end and another over two bays of the south passage-aisle. The galleries were cantilevered out in the manner of an inn at Mishima illustrated in Morse's *Japanese Homes and their Surroundings*, an unusually specific example of the Japanese influence which informed Mackintosh's playful timberwork and, later, his domestic interiors. His model for the interior as a whole, however, was a Gothic Revival church of 1885–89 in London, Holy Trinity, Latimer Road, by Norman Shaw, particularly in the steel tie-beams which break across the vaulted ceiling. Shaw's church was a single space, a pure rectangle with windowless side walls. Such rigour was beyond Mackintosh. His chancel window is off the central axis. And though the body of the church is almost a single vessel, the space leaks around the south gallery which wants to be both outside the nave (like a shallow transept) and inside (the wall-plate is carried across, blocking the upper part of the windows). It is hard to tell whether this confusion was deliberate.

From the outside the church presents a powerful, if not wholly coherent, composition of stumpy forms. The south-west tower, modelled on a picturesquely unfinished medieval church tower at Merriott

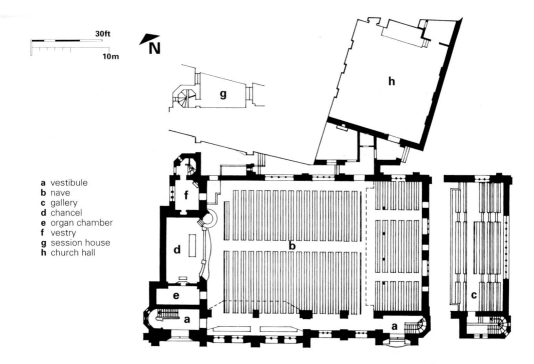

a vestibule
b nave
c gallery
d chancel
e organ chamber
f vestry
g session house
h church hall

32, 33 Queen's Cross Church, 870 Garscube Road, Glasgow, 1897–99. Plan and interior.

in Somerset which Mackintosh had sketched in 1895, has a stair turret almost growing out of it. There is a two-storey porch at the east end and a passage-aisle between the porch and the tower; the south gallery sits on top of the passage aisle like a shallow transept, with twin gables. These elements are various – the seven buttresses have three or four different slopes – and they penetrate each other. All this is Gothic, but there is no Gothic order in the design, and no room for the graceful late Gothic arcading of the churches of Shaw, Sedding or Leonard Stokes. It is as if Mackintosh had approached the design of this church with domestic architecture in mind, for crowding individual features together was exactly what Free Style architects did in their houses.

Queen's Cross Church is best seen as a treasury of details. I lived in the next street for six months and saw new details, new subtleties of surface every day. In the upper part of the east porch, for instance, we have simplified traditional mouldings in the tracery and cyma recta cap; symbolic structure in the tree-like mullion; sacred symbolism in the little bird, the Pelican in her Piety; subtle surfaces in the up-turned

35

46

34, 35 Queen's Cross Church. View from the south-west, and detail of the east porch.

chamfer of the window-head; and pure, arrogant form in the almost dangerous projection of the cap. You cannot look at this and doubt Mackintosh's talent for detail: his interest seems to focus there. But you might wonder whether his was not a purely formal talent, an appetite of the imagination which would treat all buildings in the same way, regardless of type.

The plans for Queen's Cross Church went to the local authority in June 1897. In July *The Studio* published an article by its former editor, Gleeson White, on the Macdonald sisters and Mackintosh. Another followed in September on McNair and their friend Talwin Morris. White had perhaps sensed the newness of Glasgow's decorative art at the Arts and Crafts Exhibition in 1896, and the androgynous figures in the Macdonald sisters' work may have intrigued him. (Under his editorship, *The Studio* had published articles on Beardsley and homo-erotic photography.) This 1897 article was probably influential, for *The Studio* was the principal record of progressive decorative art in Britain, and widely read in Europe. According to the Mackintosh myth, 'the attention of all revolutionary elements in the European art world was immediately focused on Scotland, on Glasgow and particularly on Mackintosh'.[14] This sounds exaggerated. And even if it is true, the revolutionary elements would have found an account of Mackintosh that was both hesitant and incomplete. *The Studio's* policy was to be avant-garde without taking risks. White's text was bland – he defended The Four's right to experiment more than the experiments themselves. And the illustrations were inadequate: Mackintosh was represented only by the Buchanan Street murals, a poster, and three pieces of furniture. These were all early experiments in decorative art. His architectural work was more mature, but it went unnoticed. Gleeson White died in 1898 and after that no other British journalist took much interest in Mackintosh. A few examples of his work appeared in *The Studio*, but little in other British periodicals.

By 1898, in any case, Mackintosh had found another champion. In October 1897 the first number of the Munich magazine *Dekorative Kunst* carried a short, unillustrated report saying that the work of Mackintosh, the Macdonald sisters, George Walton and others had given Glasgow 'a new face'.[15] By that time Mackintosh had already met Hermann Muthesius, an architect who had been attached to the German embassy in London since October 1896, studying British technical achievements, and who was to become the most influential and intelligent observer of British architecture and decorative art. In November 1897 Muthesius approached Mackintosh about publishing illustrations of his work. In November 1898 *Dekorative Kunst* carried a longer, illustrated article on The Four and Talwin Morris.[16] It was anonymous, and we do not know that it was written by Muthesius, but the points it made were typical of him. Mackintosh was represented by illustrations of furniture mainly from the mid-1890s, and the spiritual quality of The Four's work was contrasted with down-to-earth English work.

It is not surprising that Munich should have been one of the first European centres to notice decorative arts in Glasgow, for the Glasgow Boys had exhibited there with great success in the early 1890s, and the mid-1890s were a time of intense production among Munich's decorative artists, under the equally powerful influences of Art Nouveau (Peter Behrens, Otto Eckmann, August Endell, Hermann Obrist) and English Arts and Crafts (Bernhard Pankok, Richard Riemerschmid). At about the time of the second article in *Dekorative Kunst*, Mackintosh furnished the dining room of its publisher, Hugo Bruckmann, at Nymphenburgerstrasse 86 with a fitted cupboard, a

48

36 Competition design for Glasgow International Exhibition, 1898. Perspective. The original is untraced.

frieze, double doors and an elegant gun cupboard embellished with beaten metal panels probably by Margaret Macdonald.

In the middle of 1898 Mackintosh drew up Honeyman and Keppie's competition designs for Glasgow's International Exhibition. 36 This was planned to coincide with the opening of the Corporation's magnificent art gallery and museum in 1901. Competitors were asked to design an Industrial Hall, Machinery Hall and Concert Hall around the new building in Kelvingrove Park. Exhibition buildings are expected to be temporary or demountable, like the Crystal Palace of 1851. In the late 19th century they were also expected to be festive, even exotic, as the Crystal Palace in its greenhouse simplicity was not. Thus the winning design for the main building at the International Exhibition, by the Glasgow architect James Miller, was a metal structure clad in prefabricated plaster panels. Miller linked its frothy white and gold ornament with the Spanish Renaissance, though the public saw it as Oriental.

Mackintosh could have designed a building like this. In the early and mid-1890s he had shown a flair for ornamental detail, and he was no stranger to making things look other than they were. But he chose the opposite. His ribbed towers with ogee roofs and his segmental-arched windows under curved gables echo his earlier competition

49

designs, such as the railway terminus of 1892; only he replaced the intricate detail of those designs with simple, almost abstracted features in a style not easily named. It was not so much that his work was getting simpler. Another competition design of 1898, for the National Bank of Scotland buildings in Glasgow, was suitably elaborate with obvious debts to Belcher's Institute of Chartered Accountants. It was more that the make-believe, 'shopfitting' character of entertainment buildings moved him to radical simplicity rather than to frothiness. We shall see this again in his designs for tea rooms.

38 It was probably late in 1898 that Mackintosh designed a bedroom at Westdel, Dowanhill, Glasgow, for Robert Maclehose, publisher and bookseller. It was a second-floor room, 17 by 13 feet (5.2 by 3.9 metres). He ran a frieze rail, 4½ inches (11.5 centimetres) deep, round the room at door-height; divided the lower wall with uprights a little less than 4½ inches wide; and decorated the upper with a frieze. Into this grid he fitted a bed, bedside cupboard, fireplace, settle, dressing-table and wardrobe. The furniture and the intervals of the wall were based on a 3-inch (7.6-centimetre) module, and only the dressing-table stood free from the rail and uprights. The drawing of the bed, fireplace and settle shows the principal elements of the design. The wall and the furniture are integrated. The uprights are slim and elongated. Everything is white with little spots of colour. The motifs are roses and other flower forms, a tree/mannikin/phallus on the bed-end, a peacock over the fireplace, and four little squares pierced in the settle. And though the frieze is still stiff, the furniture displays the lovely curves we have seen on Mackintosh's buildings: the wave-moulding or bird's wing which complements straight lines, and the angular curve which fights against them. He probably used a flexible metal ruler or 'spring-line' to draw them in full size. It would be hard to exaggerate the historical importance of this modest room. It looks back to George Walton's interiors of the 1890s in which most of its principal elements were developed. And it looks forward to Mackintosh's mature interiors of the early 1900s on which he collaborated with Margaret Macdonald.

39 The Westdel wardrobe is as sophisticated as his building details, but in its own way. The doors are of frame-and-panel construction and the metal plaques are held in place by mouldings pinned on. But the entire surface is covered with thick layers of paint which probably include a lead-based primer used on the Clyde for filling the grain of yachts' hulls. Here the paint was rubbed down to a fine sheen. Instead of wood and framing, we see a smooth, buttery surface which does

not explain itself. With all sense of materials and construction suppressed, the way is clear for symbolic structure: the central upright runs up to a motif like a mushroom or a monk's hood, and sweeps out elegantly along the curved profile of the doors. Mackintosh could have left it at that. But his sense of humour insisted on adding straphinges of thin metal that do no work – Arts and Crafts honesty parodied in pure linear form – with eyes in their ends that glare like a warrior's in a Japanese print.

Mackintosh had a sense of humour. His buildings, and Free Style buildings generally, were often witty. And the ends of these strap hinges do look like eyes. But is there more going on? In 1898–99 Mackintosh designed Ruchill Street Free Church Halls, a small build- 37 ing with a façade more various and exciting than the accommodation warranted. I remember the first time I saw a face under the gable on the right. Now I cannot not see it. In 1902 Muthesius likened Mackintosh's furniture to 'primitive forms which stare at us with a mysterious gaze'.[17] Is this another of Mackintosh's games? Are you looking at the building, or is the building looking at you?

37 Ruchill Street Free Church Halls, Ruchill Street, Glasgow, 1898–99.

38 Design for the interior of a bedroom at Westdel, 2 Queen's Place, Dowanhill, Glasgow, probably 1898. Elevation of the south wall. Pencil and watercolour.

39 Wardrobe for the bedroom at Westdel, probably 1898. Cypress, painted off-white, with metal handles and hinge-straps, and two beaten metal panels.

40 High-backed chair for Miss Cranston's Tea Rooms, 114 Argyle Street, Glasgow, 1898–99. Oak, stained dark.

41 Design for a hat, coat and umbrella stand for Miss Cranston's Tea Rooms, 114 Argyle Street, Glasgow, 1898–99.

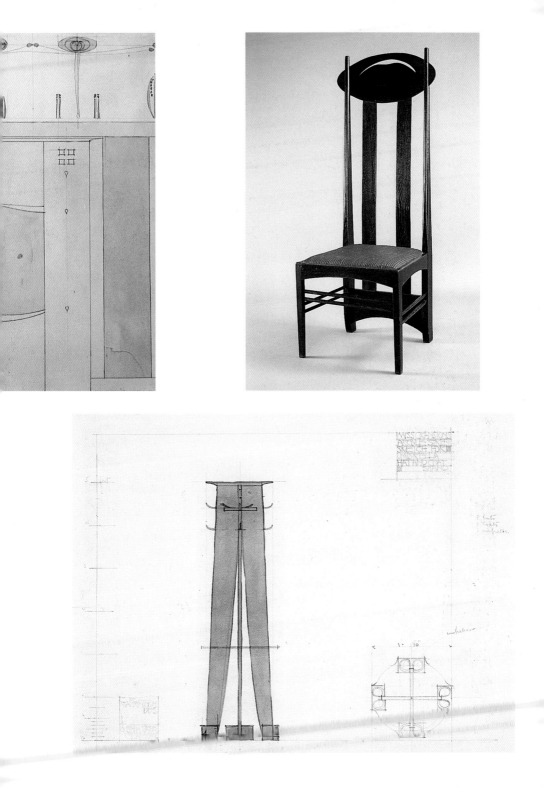

Between June 1898 and April 1899 Miss Cranston refurbished the block of buildings which contained 114 Argyle Street, where she had opened her first tea room, adding a luncheon room, and smoking and billiard rooms. This time Walton designed the decorations, Mackintosh the numerous dining chairs, armchairs, stools, settles, tables and hat stands.[18] The commission was probably carried out in Mackintosh's own name, not Honeyman and Keppie's, and it put furniture in the forefront of his work.

Unlike the early carcase furniture, or that at Westdel, the Argyle Street furniture is made of simple pieces of oak, subtly shaped, assembled in an unconventional, kit-like way, and sparingly decorated with cut-outs and carved panels. On the first of Mackintosh's high-backed chairs, the tapering back legs are rectangular in plan at the bottom, then oval, then circular. The curved oval backrail, pierced by a stylized flying bird, simply slots into the legs, and the two broader uprights, on a subtly different slope from the legs, merely touch the back of the seat as they pass. The jointing and sleight-of-hand recall the wooden fantasy constructions in his buildings, while the oval, hovering behind your head as you sit, is like a detail from a watercolour by The Four. The other pieces are much simpler, but almost as subtle. The hat stand, for instance, consists of a base, four planks and a crown, and depends for its effect on the tapering of the planks, and details like the twist in the wrought-iron loops for umbrellas. It seems as if Mackintosh rejoiced in simplicity here. We can call this his 'plank style'.

It is sometimes said that this furniture was designed for masculine areas at Argyle Street, which explains its sturdiness. But the situation is more complicated. Mackintosh did, perhaps, see the sturdy plank style as masculine (he used it on Bruckmann's gun cupboard). But all the Argyle Street furniture looks sturdy and not all of it was designed for men: the heaviest armchair was for the ladies' reading room. Taste probably mattered as much as gender here; and Mackintosh was probably aware of similar joiner-made furniture by Arts and Crafts designers such as Ford Madox Brown and Charles Spooner. Robert Lorimer, the Edinburgh architect, noted the 'artificial crudeness' of some exhibits at the Arts and Crafts Exhibition Society in 1896, and perhaps Mackintosh did too.[19]

This is perhaps the place to point out that only some of Mackintosh's furniture is strong. Sometimes the design is to blame, sometimes the workmanship, and sometimes both. One common problem is the use of dowels for joints, which do not allow for move-

42 Detail of a high-backed chair from
the Willow Tea Rooms, Glasgow, 1903,
showing the dowel construction.

ment; the dowels are sometimes harder than the wood itself and are
not grooved. This can cause splitting in Mackintosh furniture. Other
faults in design are stretchers at the same level all the way round,
which are thus weak at the joints, and feet that are not chamfered to
protect the grain from pulling. Faults in workmanship are the use of
pine on light chairs instead of ash which has more tensile strength;
crowded dowel joints; and standard joinery screws instead of the
special cabinet-makers' kind.[20] In fact, the methods of construction in
Mackintosh's furniture are often those of the joiner and shop-fitter
rather than the cabinet-maker, which poses a small historical problem,
for almost the only makers' names we have are Francis Smith and
Alexander Martin, who produced a lot of the furniture. Both advertised themselves as cabinet-makers.

All during these years, Glasgow School of Art was being built under
Keppie's supervision. On 20 December 1899, in light rain, the new
building was opened. Newbery's younger daughter Mary presented
the key on a white cushion and Keppie spoke on behalf of the architects. When the ceremony was over, the assembled company
inspected the building. They could see the Headmaster's room, and
the light-filled board room where the curves of the windows and their
panelled embrasures form one undulating, insubstantial wall; with the
bedroom at Westdel, these were Mackintosh's first white rooms. They
saw the artificial crudeness of the roughly sawn timbers which panel
the corridors, and the little panels of stained glass in many of the doors

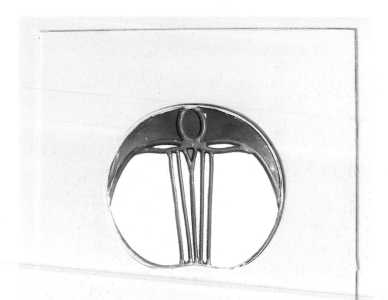

43 Stained-glass panel
in a cupboard in the
Headmaster's room,
Glasgow School of
Art, *c.* 1899.

43   with their abstract-organic motifs: seeds, trees, birds, roses. In the
evening the students held two concerts and a dance. Margaret
Macdonald was there, her auburn hair 'well set off' as one paper said,
by her fawn dress.[21]

We do not know what Mackintosh felt on this occasion, but his
thoughts may have turned to the question of recognition. It was ten
years since he had joined Honeyman and Keppie as a draughtsman,
and he was beginning to be known for work done in his own name.
It was right that Keppie should be acknowledged, for he had been
responsible for the work of building the School. But the design,
which was so singular, was Mackintosh's. In 1898 he had told
Muthesius: 'I hope when brighter days come, I shall be able to work
for myself entirely and claim my work as mine.'[22]

That he was a designer of a different order from Keppie was apparent in two buildings which he worked on in the early months of 1900.
44,45   One was a newspaper printing office for *The Daily Record*, a young
and technically progressive Glasgow paper, on a narrow rectangular

56

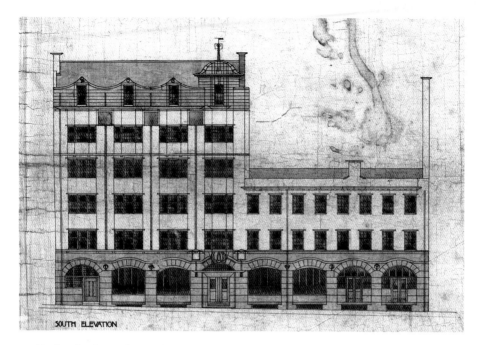

SOUTH ELEVATION

44 Design for the *Daily Record* building, 20–28 Renfield Lane, Glasgow, 1900–1901, 1903–4. Elevation to Renfield Lane, April 1900.

site in Renfield Lane. The planning and construction of the *Daily Record* building are conventional. Interest is focused, as so often with Mackintosh, on the façade. The basement and first three floors of the whole building were erected between July 1900 and May 1901, and occupied by the newspaper; the upper storeys on the left were built between November 1903 and May 1904. Mackintosh's façade, on the other hand, treated the right side of the printing works as a mere annexe, and the left as a single Free Style composition. The five-storey oriel over the entrance recalls the interpenetrating forms of the east wing of the School of Art, while the fourth-floor oriels and the attic details have the same Scottish Baronial top-heaviness as the upper stages of the *Glasgow Herald* building. Renfield Lane was only 18 feet (5.5 metres) wide and, to get more light into the alley, Mackintosh clothed his façade in white glazed bricks, as if it were a light well. He then enlivened this facing with green- and red-glazed bricks in the form of stylized trees, closely modelled on the Tree of Life motifs on the east elevation of the Passmore Edwards Settlement in London.

25

12

45 *Daily Record* building. Detail of the ground-floor arcade.

46 Fireplace at Threave Castle, Kirkcudbrightshire. From MacGibbon and Ross, *The Castellated and Domestic Architecture of Scotland* (Edinburgh 1887), vol. 1.

45   The ground floor was treated as a sequence of segmental arches, each with a generous cyma recta profile. At the apex of the arch, where one might expect the compressed mass of a keystone, the fillet is drawn down into a kind of tongue, light, open and graceful, which both interrupts and continues the curve of the arch. At the imposts, on the other hand, where the arches meet the piers, there are massive blocks, unmoulded and ignorant of curves. There is no evidence that they were meant to be carved. They are brutal and repeated stops to the flow of the arcade. Over the entrance architrave, two smaller segmental mouldings have been penetrated by a keystone and the corbel of the five-storey oriel – yet they are in equipoise, weight and mass held by lightness and line. The balance depends on the underside of the keystone being curved. This little fantasia seems to be based on the relationship between lintel and relieving arch in Scottish buildings

46   of the 17th century and earlier; one example in *The Castellated and Domestic Architecture of Scotland* also includes a keystone. Here we see the growing sophistication of Mackintosh's detail. It is, by comparison with the *Glasgow Herald* building, fluent and economical, simpler to the eye, but much more complex to the mind.

    The other new building was a detached middle-class house, of the sort that could be found in fashionable late Victorian suburbs and commuter villages in many parts of Britain. In the design of such buildings, Free Style architects would draw on the imagery of old farmhouses and manor-houses, using informal plans, traditional materials and a show of ingenuity; the Free Style amounted, in domestic architecture, to a Vernacular Revival. The owners of these buildings could see their homes as individual, unassuming, and proper to the countryside. Muthesius thought this type represented 'the best in contemporary English architectural practice'.[23]

Mackintosh's client was William Davidson, a Glasgow provisions merchant who combined Presbyterian integrity with progressive tastes, and the house was to be built on a site that gave it the name Windyhill, above the village of Kilmacolm, 14 miles (22.5 kilometres) west of Glasgow. The middle-class houses which lined the leafy roads of Kilmacolm after the arrival of the railway were, in some cases, Scottish in style, with turreted skylines. But most were English, showing the powerfully English origins of the Vernacular Revival. Mackintosh cut through this uncertainty by building Davidson's house of rubble faced with harling (which the English 47 call roughcast). Harling belonged both to Scottish building traditions and to English Vernacular Revival taste: Voysey's roughcast houses were well-known. It also lent itself to Mackintosh's peculiar purposes.

In Scotland, harling was particularly associated with the 16th- and 17th-century houses of the lesser gentry, such as Lamb's House at Leith, with their small, deep-set windows scattered in an expanse of wall; their shallow recessions and overhangs in the plane of the wall; their openings cut into the thickness of the wall often without any dressing or margin; and their general freedom of massing which is made all the more telling by the uniform covering. All these features can be seen on Windyhill, signalling a new departure in Mackintosh's work. Until now, he had never designed a building so clearly dependent on a single historical type, or one without mouldings, or one whose light, uniform skin threw so much attention on the mass. He may have learned from the harled cottages and estate buildings at Fortingall, Perthshire, designed by James Maclaren and his successors Dunn and Watson in 1889–92 in an austere and angular version of the Scottish vernacular, and from Robert Lorimer's calmer harled cottages of the 1890s at Colinton, near Edinburgh.

The plan of Windyhill is L-shaped, like many Vernacular Revival 48 houses, with the reception rooms ranged off a long hall and the principal bedrooms above, facing south-west over the village of Kilmacolm towards Duchal Moor; the service wing runs off to the

47 View from the north-east.

Windyhill, Houston Street,
Kilmacolm, Renfrewshire,
1900–1901

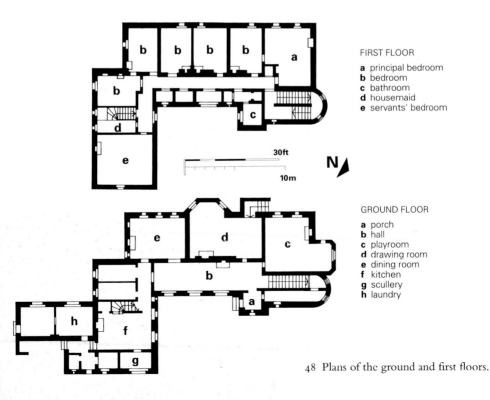

FIRST FLOOR

a principal bedroom
b bedroom
c bathroom
d housemaid
e servants' bedroom

30ft

10m

N

GROUND FLOOR

a porch
b hall
c playroom
d drawing room
e dining room
f kitchen
g scullery
h laundry

48 Plans of the ground and first floors.

north-east under a slightly lower roof. The elevations are austere, particularly the garden front, and Davidson was twitted on the morning
train to Glasgow about the prison he had built. But it was a defensive
austerity, suited to a windy hillside in Scotland, and the daily life of
the Davidsons could make it homely. It was often claimed as a merit
in these houses that they were 'honest', that their elevations were a
direct and unaffected expression of their plans, and Windyhill has
some of this quality. But Mackintosh was too clever, too fond of
complexity, to be merely honest. He created careful (and honest-
seeming) asymmetry on the garden front by depriving the left-hand
room on the first floor of a window facing south-west, complexity at
the north-east corner of the service wing by bringing a great catslide
roof down over the lobby and lavatory, where a simple gabled outshut
would have done as well, and a medley of overlapping and interpenetrating forms round the entrance, where the main wing seems to
be eating the porch: the left-hand jamb of the entrance is already
halfway in. These are Mackintosh's peculiar purposes: in the cubic,
interpenetrating forms round the entrance, clothed in harling,
Mackintosh's admiration for the Scottish vernacular and his growing
love of abstraction are indistinguishable.

49 Design for the garden front,
1900. Pencil and wash.

50 The main entrance.

Mackintosh was thirty-two when he designed Windyhill. He had reached maturity as an architect during one of the most fruitful decades in Glasgow's architectural history, when the new buildings of the city were generally Free Style in character, Northern, and particularly Scottish, Renaissance in vocabulary, and free and inventive in detail. In the city centre, commercial prosperity, narrow sites and generous building regulations had encouraged an almost American vigour and verticality. Mackintosh's principal buildings of the decade – a warehouse, an art school, a church, a printing office and a private house – were typical. We have seen their debts to Scottish Baronial and the Free Style, though we have not seen quite how heavily Mackintosh drew on a small number of English Free Style architects. About half the contemporary buildings cited as sources in this chapter were published in the form of special plates in *The Architect* by the Architectural Illustration Society, an élite of London architects centred around the pupils and assistants of Shaw, Belcher and Sedding; these were the architects with whom had allied himself in 1893.

At the same time, Mackintosh's work stood out. The *Glasgow Herald* building and Queen's Cross Church stood out because of their detail, 'novel to the verge of eccentricity' as *The Builders' Journal* wrote in 1895.[24] The discontinuities in the design of Glasgow School of Art revealed a much deeper originality which seeks to engage with the spectator's own perceptions, something perhaps unparalleled in Britain at this date. And though the Ruchill Street Free Church Halls, the *Daily Record* building and Windyhill were much less radical than the School of Art, they demonstrated Mackintosh's growing and unusual ability to speak in elevations: the liveliness of their exteriors was generated by something other than the plan.

The architectural historian John Archer has written that Mackintosh lacked 'that large command of plan and structure that belongs to architects of absolutely the first rank', and the office building at 142a–144 St Vincent Street, designed in 1899 by Mackintosh's small and opinionated friend James Salmon, illustrates the point.[25] Salmon's detail was like Mackintosh's – vivid natural forms round the entrance, and deep, simplified cornices breaking forward over slim piers. But his overall treatment was not. There was no concentration on detail, no discontinuity, no playing games with our perceptions, just the clear articulation of a ten-storey façade, the stonework pared away to maximize light, the verticals able to embrace variations from floor to floor. We have not found such clarity in Mackintosh's work. But its absence is a clue to his purposes, not a measure of his failure.

51

51 James Salmon the Younger:
142a–144 St Vincent Street,
Glasgow, 1899–1902.

He was not looking for breadth or coherence, but for a kind of generative looseness, the parts shifting in relation to each other and to the
observer. He was more like a conjurer than a commander.

During the second half of the 1890s, art and reputation, the subsidiary themes of this chapter, came to the fore. Working with the
Macdonald sisters and McNair uncovered a symbolic side to
Mackintosh's imagination which Honeyman and Keppie might never
have brought to light. He might have gone on designing buildings,
and simply painted symbolic watercolours on the side. But he had a
special talent for designing in three dimensions, provided the job was
small and the structural constraints few, and it was here that his
imagination began to work, in a middle ground between art and
architecture: first on wooden fantasies inside his buildings, then on
furniture and interiors.

And so, in the second half of the 1890s, the decorative arts took a
larger place in his work. And in his reputation. It was Mackintosh the
decorative artist who exhibited with the Arts and Crafts Exhibition
Society and figured in *The Studio* and *Dekorative Kunst*, not

63

Mackintosh the architect. Since the 18th century, it had been usual for style-conscious architects to be involved in the decorative arts, either as an extension of their architectural work (getting the furnishings right) or as the exercise of different, complementary skills. Mackintosh's posters, furniture and interiors were at first complementary. They did not arise from his architecture and did not, at this stage, extend it. They arose from his own imaginative explorations.

And they were sustained by contemporary movements in the decorative arts. The idealism of the Arts and Crafts movement made the decorative arts particularly attractive to progressive architects all over Britain. In Glasgow middle-class prosperity, Newbery's emphasis on the teaching of design and craft at the School of Art, and the need to fit out luxury liners on the Clyde, had created a flourishing network of furnishers, decorators and designer-craftsmen. During the 1890s progressive design in the city developed a style of its own, rooted in admiration for the painter James McNeill Whistler and the Aesthetic Movement, but influenced by Symbolism and Art Nouveau. Light, unified interiors, elongated, curving forms, stylized mouldings, green, rose-pink and purple as favourite colours, and much use of stencilling and stained glass were pioneered by George Walton early in the 1890s. They were taken up by Mackintosh later in the decade. And in the early 1900s they were popularized as the Glasgow Style.

Working with the Macdonald sisters and McNair also uncovered Mackintosh's capacity for love. The early relationship between Mackintosh and Margaret Macdonald is not well documented, but they were perhaps thought of as a pair by 1897: writing to Muthesius in November, Mackintosh ended his letter 'With kind regards from Miss Macdonald and myself.'[26] On 22 August 1900 the two were married in the Episcopal church at Dumbarton. He was working-class, industrious, good with children, perhaps a little morose, and quick to fly into a rage; but he had a disarming taste for simple things and was capable of great kindness. She was middle-class, three years older than him, and stately, with a mass of auburn hair. Mackintosh's niece Margaret recalled that, as a child, she found her aunt condescending and aloof, but she added: 'I remember thinking that they must love each other. I don't know why but I just thought that.'[27]

Margaret's father was a Scottish mining engineer, her mother was English, and she had grown up in England, in the Midlands. The family came to Glasgow in the late 1880s, and Margaret and her sister Frances enrolled at Glasgow School of Art, where both shone, Frances more brightly than Margaret. They left the school in 1894 and took

52 Margaret Macdonald Mackintosh, photographed by T. & R. Annan *c.* 1902.

a studio at 128 Hope Street where they worked together, often col-
laboratively. In June 1899 Frances married Herbert McNair and they
went to live in Liverpool, where McNair was an instructor in the
School of Architecture and Applied Art at University College. We do
not know when Margaret got engaged to Mackintosh (like all their
friends she called him 'Tosh' or 'Toshie'). Nor do we know much
about their life together or their affections, until almost the end of
Mackintosh's life. But this much is clear: Mackintosh and Margaret
Macdonald came together not only as man and woman, but also as
artists. From this point on, the story of Mackintosh's life, and of his
work, cannot be told as if he were a single person.

CHAPTER THREE

Love and Work
Mains Street 1900–1906

In this chapter, we will lose sight of Mackintosh as an architect for a few years, as furniture and interiors take up much of his time. This is a change of scene. In the 1890s he was a young man, exploring the outside world, and finding his own direction. Now, for a time, he turns inward and enters an intimate and largely domestic world. The vehicle of his imagination is the room, an enclosing or embracing space, and he works with light, colour, imagery and malleable, non-structural materials. These were the early years of Mackintosh's marriage and they were, perhaps, the most creative period of his life. It is as if Margaret Macdonald took him by the hand and they went inside together. In this chapter the associations of 'interior' include inwardness, sexual intimacy and the decoration of a house.

Round the beginning of 1900, they had furnished and decorated 53 the first-floor flat in which they would live. No. 120 Mains Street was an early Victorian building with high ceilings, crisp cornices and big Glasgow windows to maximize the light. The two largest rooms became a drawing room and a studio. In the drawing room they 54, 55 divided the walls with uprights and a frieze rail which ran right round the room and across the windows, apart from tiny interruptions to preserve the window architraves. The fireplace, whose massive, simple forms look like masonry, was actually made of light planks, perhaps boxing in an existing fireplace. The windows were hung with fine muslin, and the background colours were quiet: grey carpet, light grey canvas on the lower wall, white paint on the upper, woodwork enamelled white. But there were little spots of colour: purple squares in the frieze, and purple glass in the gas-light fittings which hung level with the frieze rail, in clusters of four. The bookcase glazed with cream-coloured and purple glass and a white-painted and richly modelled desk were new, and so was the big, box-like chair with stylized 52 trees in which Margaret was photographed. The rest of the furniture was a scatter of existing Mackintosh designs. There were Japanese prints propped against the walls, and arrangements of dried clematis that recall the swirling lines of Margaret's paintings.

a hall
b dining room
c drawing room
d studio
e kitchen
f bedroom
g principal bedroom
h maid's room

30ft

10m

N

53 No. 120 Mains Street, Glasgow. Conjectural reconstruction of the plan of the Mackintoshes' flat. The studio, drawing room and dining room are based on early photographs and the fabric surviving in the late 1980s; the kitchen is based on the fabric in the late 1980s; and the two bedrooms are inferred from the fabric of the floor above in the late 1980s. (Based on a drawing by Bill Roger)

The dining room was much smaller, and dark. The walls were 56 covered with a plain, grey-brown paper below the frieze rail, and the woodwork was stained dark. In photographs, the effect is almost sepulchral under the white frieze and ceiling. It was common in late 19th-century middle-class houses for the drawing room and bedrooms, which were thought of as feminine, to be light in colour, while the dining room, study, billiard room and smoking room, which were thought of as masculine, would be sober, even dark. For some years from 1900, male and female, light and dark became primary and fruitful oppositions in the Mackintoshes' work.

54–56 No. 120 Mains Street. Two views of the drawing room (*opposite*), and the dining room, all photographed in March 1900.

The bedroom was also small, and crowded with furniture. There 57 were two cupboards with elaborately modelled doors, a large four-poster bed and an extraordinary cheval mirror. The room was all 58 white, but the hangings of the bed were enriched with colour. There were coloured panels in the frieze rail, and glass in the foot of the bed which threw coloured light on the newly married couple. Since 1895, it seems, Mackintosh had been living in his bachelor's den in the basement of his father's house, with dark paper on the walls, a strange frieze of cats, and a big bed stained green. Now, answering to

69

57 Margaret's imagination, he designed a bed like a white bower, a place of intimacy, celebration and perhaps of innocence.

Near the top of the cheval mirror are two delicate, tendril-like motifs ending in leaves or buds of pink glass. Elsewhere at Mains Street there were birds on the bedroom cupboards, a peacock's tail on the desk, branches and pod-like forms on the bookcase. Muthesius thought that these linear motifs all had a meaning.[1] Some represent particular objects like a rose, and have particular meanings to do with sexuality; others look like several things at once, and can be understood as the lines of nature. They took their shape from the conventional treatment of natural forms taught in late 19th-century art schools, and their meaning from the symbolic language of The Four. They are organic, lines of life, and they add a living and sometimes almost human quality to furniture. For the Mackintoshes they were sensuous and intensely personal, and were not, perhaps, quite so convincing when used on other people's furniture.

The design historian David Brett has written that the curve of the 58 cheval mirror is that of a female hip and pelvic girdle thrust forward,

57 No. 120 Mains Street. The bedroom in March 1900.

making it Margaret's mirror, a private and erotic thing.[2] The resemblance may be fanciful. But Mains Street certainly was a withdrawn, sensuous and self-conscious place. All the objects in the flat were familiar – cupboards, tables, chairs – but they had been worked over by Mackintosh's formal and Margaret's Romantic imagination and given new dimensions, spatial and spiritual. They are both welcoming and strange. Nowadays they are shown in the interiors of 6 Florentine Terrace, which have been reconstructed at the Hunterian Art Gallery in Glasgow; visitors wait until the attendant looks away, and then touch them, stroking the silky surfaces as they would stroke a lover, exploring, looking for reassurance. 124, 125

There were several, sometimes contradictory, levels of meaning at Mains Street. It was a respectable middle-class flat, in which late Victorian conventions of privacy and domestic ritual were brought to a new level of intensity. Yet its sparseness challenged middle-class taste. Some things may have been cleared away for the photographer, but there was surely never the warm clutter of late Victorian domestic life: no bric-a-brac, no banks of family photographs on the tables, not even mementos, it seems, of the life which either Mackintosh or Margaret had lived before. Everything was art. The plain walls and the careful placing of the twig arrangements recalled the paintings of Whistler and domestic interiors in Japan. There was a kind of luxury in the modelled details of the furniture, and critics called the spots of colour 'gem-like'. But in fact the materials were cheap – enamel, glass or coloured stones – for it was art, not wealth, which was on display.

It was coherent, in the sense that the furniture and interior decoration formed a single scheme. As we shall see later, Muthesius thought Mackintosh was almost the only Briton to understand the idea of a room as a work of art.[3] Yet it was also a compromise. The original photographs show early Victorian rooms into which a turn-of-the-century interior has been carefully fitted. Mackintosh did not lower the ceiling or block out the upper part of the windows to get his horizontals. He knew how to articulate space, but he left the large undifferentiated drawing room alone. He had no particular love for early Victorian detail, but he left all the cornices and architraves intact. Today, a conservation architect might work in this way; but Mackintosh, though he liked complexity, was not like that. It may be that he was not allowed to alter the fabric, and that is why the drawing-room frieze rail stops at the architraves. He was, after all, only a tenant. At Mains Street, he was not quite in a position to create the room as a work of art.

Contemporaries were struck by the intense atmosphere of Mains Street. It seemed impossibly pure. Muthesius called it a 'fairy-tale world' in which 'a book in an unsuitable binding would disturb the atmosphere simply by lying on the table'.[4] And it was very personal: a French writer, E. B. Kalas, described it as a place of virginal beauty inhabited by 'two visionary souls in ecstatic communion'.[5] They seemed like the emanations of their own designs. And even today, in the Hunterian Art Gallery, visitors respond by recreating Mackintosh and Margaret in their minds.

In fact, we know little about the Mackintoshes' personal lives at this time. We can imagine Margaret in the soft light, turning the pages of a verse-drama by Maeterlinck, sharing some subtlety of thought with her husband; but we are only imagining. We do not know whether they lived the kind of life their furniture suggests. Seventy years later, Mary Sturrock, Francis Newbery's younger daughter, recalled this interior, and that of Florentine Terrace, in a single happy image. 'The house was always so pretty and fresh. But what seems to come across is that they were so awfully nice. A bright red glowing fire, the right sort of cake, a nice tea, and kind hearts – and a lot of fun.'[6]

In the first half of 1900, while they were preparing Mains Street, Mackintosh and Margaret were also working on their first big tea-room interior for Miss Cranston. Tea rooms had their beginnings in Glasgow of the 1870s, when they catered mainly for businessmen and were clustered around the Merchant City. Influenced but not dominated by the temperance movement, they served lunches and teas, good cheap food in clean and pleasant surroundings. Soon they were also patronized by women. Homeliness was often the keynote of their interiors, but some were also self-consciously artistic, placing themselves in the late Victorian woman's realm of art and the home. They grew in numbers in the 1890s, expanding westwards towards the fashionable shopping streets and department stores, and Miss Cranston's premises in Buchanan Street and Argyle Street were among the most artistic of these, and pioneers of their type. For Mackintosh and Margaret, who were shaping their own version of art and domesticity, a tea-room commission could not have been more timely.

59–62 The new interior was an addition to Miss Cranston's Ingram Street tea rooms, in the heart of the Merchant City. In 1886 she had opened a tea room at 205 Ingram Street, on the ground floor of a warehouse- and office-block, adding a lunch room at 209–211 in 1888. Now, to make a ladies' lunch room, a new billiard room and and a smoking room, she had taken on 213–215, two shops that had been thrown into

58 The cheval mirror from 120 Mains Street, 1900, in the reconstructed bedroom at the Hunterian Art Gallery, Glasgow. Oak, painted white, with coloured glass panels and white metal handles.

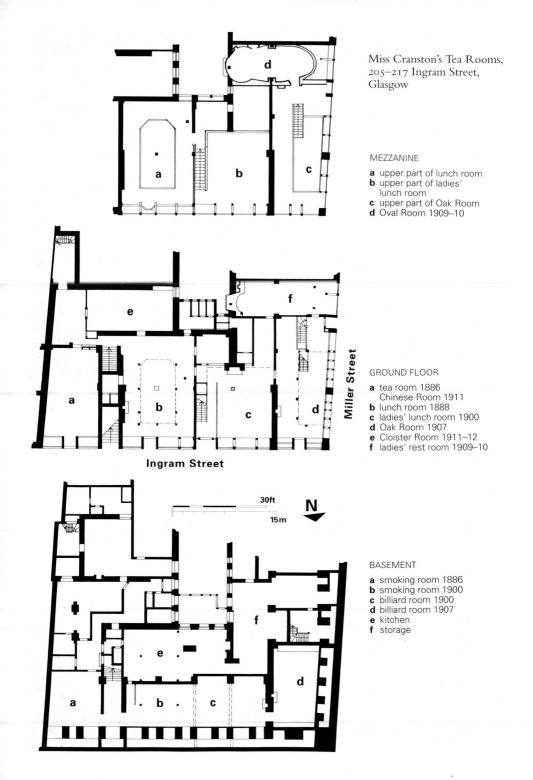

Miss Cranston's Tea Rooms,
205–217 Ingram Street,
Glasgow

MEZZANINE

a upper part of lunch room
b upper part of ladies'
lunch room
c upper part of Oak Room
d Oval Room 1909–10

Miller Street

Ingram Street

GROUND FLOOR

a tea room 1886
Chinese Room 1911
b lunch room 1888
c ladies' lunch room 1900
d Oak Room 1907
e Cloister Room 1911–12
f ladies' rest room 1909–10

30ft

15m

N

BASEMENT

a smoking room 1886
b smoking room 1900
c billiard room 1900
d billiard room 1907
e kitchen
f storage

one in about 1889 with a big column in the middle carrying the floor above. For the ladies' lunch room Mackintosh introduced full-height windows, carrying the wall above on pairs of columns which suggest a gap between the outside of the building and the inside; designed new stairs and balustrading for a gallery; screened off the tables; and panelled the room to a height of about 10 feet (3 metres), running the cornice of the panelling across the front of the windows as at Mains Street. On either side the frieze was filled with gesso panels, one by Margaret and the other by Mackintosh. All this shopfitting was done without regard to the big column on whose structural contribution this all depended; skimpily detailed, it stood in between the fireplace and the customers, and awkwardly close to the screen.

62

61

59 Plans of the basement, ground and mezzanine floors, showing the phases of Mackintosh's work in 1900, 1907, 1909–10 and 1911–2. The details of the kitchens and the storage areas at the back of the basement are conjectural.

60 The ladies' lunch room seen from the gallery, 1900.

61 Detail of the panelling, pay desk and part of the structural column.

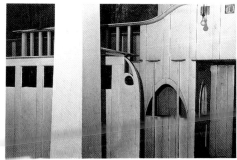

62 Miss Cranston's Tea Rooms, 205–215 Ingram Street. *The Wassail*, a panel designed and made by Mackintosh of hessian, gesso, string, glass, beads and metal, 1900.

62   The memorable gesso panels were big expanses of rough, hessian-like material all but covered with coloured gesso, with string used to define figures and trees, careful modelling of the flesh areas, and coloured glass, beads and metal applied. They showed groups of stylized women in the manner of The Four. When they were illustrated in *The Studio* in 1903, Margaret's was called *The May Queen* and Mackintosh's *The Wassail*, as if they evoked pagan festivals of summer and winter. But at Ingram Street they did not have titles, and Mackintosh's panel showed no cup, no wassailing, to help the spectator. They may have held definite meanings for their designers. But to Miss Cranston's customers they must have seemed simply decorative, pictures of Fair Women which intensified the atmosphere of the ladies' lunch room.

The Ingram Street interiors were installed between August and November 1900, so that they followed the fitting-out of the Mains Street flat. The men's billiard room and smoking room in the basement were panelled in dark wood, while the ladies' lunch room was like a well of veiled light, pierced by spots of colour and overlooked by dreaming women. The Mackintoshes had transposed their heightened version of light, feminine spaces into a place of public refreshment, and produced a room which must have seemed remarkable by comparison with other artistic tea rooms, simple and yet mysterious. But there was something missing. The private meanings had slipped from the gesso panels. The personal intensity of Mains Street would not bear translation to a public place. It was to be some years before the Mackintoshes achieved the quite different kind of intensity, impersonal and slightly overstated, that was appropriate to a tea room.

76

In the summer of 1900 the Mackintoshes and the McNairs were invited to take part in the eighth exhibition of the Vienna Secession, opening in November. Nowadays, Vienna is so much accepted as a birthplace of European Modernism that we can forget how culturally isolated it was round 1900. In 1897, various artists who were eager to be in touch with progressive art in the rest of Europe broke away from the Künstlerhaus, the established exhibiting body, and formed the Secession. They called their magazine *Ver Sacrum*, 'The Sacred Spring', for they were consciously seeking renewal. Early exhibitions included work by German, French, Belgian and British painters, and the Glasgow Boys preceded Mackintosh here as they had in Munich. The winter exhibition of 1900 was also to be international and, according to the architect Josef Hoffmann who was the driving force behind it, 'an overall view of modern handicrafts'.[7] The main

63 The Mackintoshes' exhibit at the eighth exhibition of the Vienna Secession, November 1900. From *Ver Sacrum*, vol. 3, 1900. The large panel in the frieze is Margaret Macdonald Mackintosh's *The May Queen*.

exhibition space was designed by Hoffmann, but the Mackintoshes asked to be allowed to design their own setting, and they were invited to Vienna to supervise its installation.

We have seen at Mains Street how the interior itself, rather than individual pieces, was at the heart of the Mackintoshes' collaboration. In Vienna they painted the three-sided space white, and divided the walls with tapering posts and a frieze rail. There were framed water-colours and book illustrations on the walls, and the Ingram Street panels faced each other above the rail. Some of the furniture was new and some came from Mains Street, as did the slightly precious atmos-phere: a tall, thin vase, square in plan and containing an austere spray of twigs, stood in the middle, defining the space.

It is part of the Mackintosh myth – perhaps the central part – that he was acclaimed in Vienna in 1900 and thereafter exercised a pow-erful influence in the city. Thomas Howarth told the story that, on their arrival in Vienna, the Mackintoshes were drawn through the streets by students in a flower-decked carriage, and he continued: 'Instead of grudging acknowledgement, or outspoken condemnation, he received unstinted praise, and his work was widely acclaimed by artists and public alike.'[8] Howarth went on to argue that, as a result of the Mackintoshes' exhibit, 'the entire Viennese movement, with Hoffmann at its head, blazed into new life, and the next three or four years saw the outpouring of a quantity of decorative work and fur-nishing of a very high order, all in its whiteness and plainness bearing a striking superficial resemblance to that of Mackintosh.'[9] Further, it has been argued that the decorative use of squares, which was a *leit-motif* of Viennese design in the early 20th century, was learned from Mackintosh.[10]

It would not be surprising if the Mackintoshes were welcomed in Vienna, for the sphere of work for progressive artists, architects and designers in that city was no longer the great public buildings of the Ringstrasse, but private, bourgeois domestic life – precisely the sphere of the Mackintoshes. And it is clear from the pages of *Ver Sacrum* that Secession artists, led by Gustav Klimt, were keenly interested in Symbolist figure painting.

And there is evidence to support the myth. The *Neues Wiener Tagblatt* counted the Mackintoshes' exhibit 'among the most striking achievements which modern art has created', and the *Wiener Rundschau* commented: 'There is a Christlike mood in this interior: this chair might have belonged to a Francis of Assisi.'[11] There are no reliable published accounts of the Mackintoshes' visit, but we can fairly suppose that they were welcomed by the Secession, especially its champions of the decorative arts, Hoffmann and Kolo Moser. According to one critic, the Mackintoshes were 'the guests whom our Vienna artists have probably taken closest to their hearts', and later Mackintosh was reported as saying that the trip to Vienna was the high point of his life.[12]

What is more, one can see specific examples of the Mackintoshes' influence in Vienna after 1900. In 1901 Anton Popischil Jr exhibited a high-backed chair like the Argyle Street ones; in 1902 Kolo Moser created a room-setting for the fifteenth Secession exhibition closely modelled on the Mackintoshes'; Gustav Klimt's work with its flattened, dreaming figures may owe something to the Mackintoshes' gesso panels; and some of Hoffmann's furniture is close to Mackintosh's, including some pieces made by the Wiener Werkstätte, the luxury craft workshop which he set up with Moser in 1903.[13]

But there is also evidence which shows that the Mackintoshes did not receive unstinted praise in Vienna. The critics responded to the symbolic and spiritual aspects of the Mackintoshes' work, but they generally found them more sinister than the *Wiener Rundschau* had: 'This hellish room . . . no better than a torture chamber'; 'The foreign "Moderns" are already debauched . . . they indulge in . . . prehistoric magic charms . . . furniture as fetishes' – thus wrote Hermann Bahr and Frank Servaes.[14] Ludwig Hevesi, Vienna's most articulate critic, reflected that 'The artists themselves would hardly spend their daily lives in such apartments, but they may perhaps have a haunted room in their house, a hobgoblin's closet, or something like that'; and though he thought that 'behind the foolery there is a remarkable talent', he did not see any sign of a new style in this interior.[15] These were not the words of Philistines or conservatives. Bahr, Servaes and Hevesi were three of Vienna's most progressive critics, and champions of the Secession in the daily press.

And Mackintosh's influence in Vienna has been exaggerated. There are individual instances. But from before 1900, the general direction of progressive Viennese design had been away from the structural curves of German *Jugendstil* towards simple but sophisticated rectilinear forms, and in furniture towards a dark and sober treatment increasingly influenced by early 19th-century Biedermeier designs. The process was complete by about 1903. Neither Mackintosh nor the Scottish exhibit of 1900 altered or affected this development. Josef Hoffmann was indeed at its head. And the difference between Hoffmann's work and Mackintosh's is obvious in the study of Dr

EMPFANGS·=·RAUM·UND·MUSIK·=·ZIMMER· PANELS VON MARGARET·MACDONALD· MACKINTOSH·

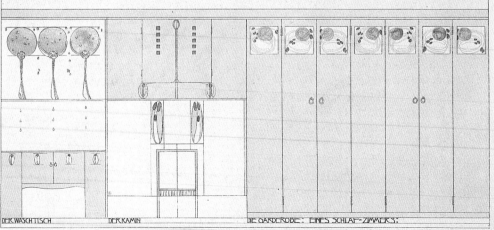

DER·WASCHTISCH· DER·KAMIN· DIE·GARDEROBE·EINES·SCHLAF·ZIMMERS·

66 The study of Dr Hugo Henneberg's house in Vienna, by Josef Hoffmann, 1901. From *Das Interieur*, vol. 4, 1903.

Hugo Henneberg's house, which Hoffmann designed in 1901: on the 66 right is a smoker's cabinet by Mackintosh, bought at the 1900 exhibition, with elegant curves, carved decoration and beaten metal panels by Margaret Macdonald, on the left a simple, rectilinear desk designed by Hoffmann. Of course, Mackintosh did design in this simple, rectilinear way; but not until later. For the truth is that it was the Viennese who inspired Mackintosh more than the other way about, as we shall see. And as for the decorative use of squares, it is clear that Hoffmann and Moser were familiar with this well before they saw it in Mackintosh's work.[16]

While they were in Vienna, the Mackintoshes may have heard of a competition for the design of a large country house for an art-lover or connoisseur. It was organized by the Darmstadt publisher Alexander Koch, and announced in December 1900 with a deadline of 25 March 1901. The house was to be distinctly modern, and the assumption was that the art should consist in the house itself, not in a house with a picture-gallery attached. This was part of the

64 A House for an Art Lover, 1901. Perspective of the drawing room and music room. Plate 7 from *Meister der Innenkunst: Charles Rennie Mackintosh, Glasgow: Haus eines Kunstfreundes*, published by Alexander Koch in Darmstadt in 1902.

65 Elevation of the west wall of the main bedroom in the House for an Art Lover, re-used in the main bedroom at Windyhill. Plate 11 from *Meister der Innenkunst,*

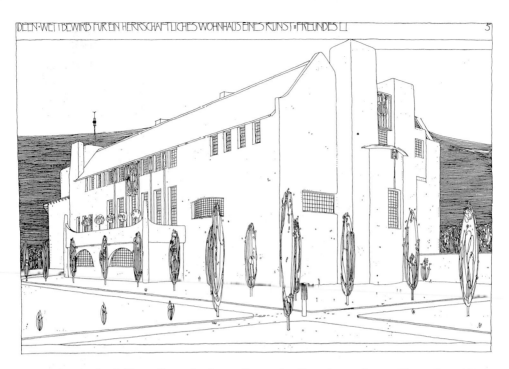

67 A House for an Art Lover. Perspective from the south-east. Plate 5 from *Meister der Innenkunst*

Mackintoshes' modernism, and they submitted an entry under the title *Der Vogel*, 'The Bird'. There were thirty-six entries, but the Mackintoshes' could not be considered, because they failed to send three perspectives of the interior. For the rest, the judges were disappointed, gave no first prize, awarded the second to the English architect M. H. Baillie Scott, and split the third three ways. When the Mackintoshes had completed their entry, Koch published their
64,65 drawings, as he did Scott's and Leopold Bauer's, as a set of fourteen
67 lithographed plates.

The Mackintoshes' design was like a more luxurious version of Windyhill and faced with harling. This was crucial, not as a building material, but as a material to be drawn. By 1900 Mackintosh could convey mass in perspective with the simplest outlines. Here, in two perspectives, he presented the house as a group of uniform white masses, with only a slight flecking to indicate texture. Overlapping and interpenetrating forms were even more important than at

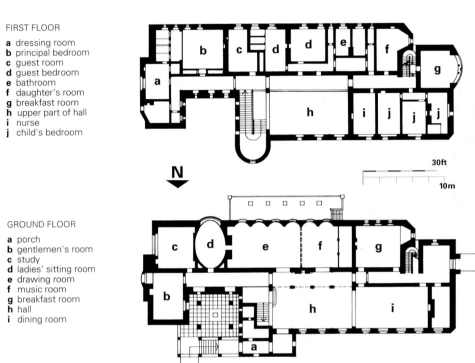

68 A House for an Art Lover. Plans of
the ground, first and attic floors.

ATTIC

a children's playroom

FIRST FLOOR

a dressing room
b principal bedroom
c guest room
d guest bedroom
e bathroom
f daughter's room
g breakfast room
h upper part of hall
i nurse
j child's bedroom

N

30ft

10m

GROUND FLOOR

a porch
b gentlemen's room
c study
d ladies' sitting room
e drawing room
f music room
g breakfast room
h hall
i dining room

Windyhill, and Mackintosh drew them with a clarity that the actual structure could never have achieved. This was a loosely planned, Free Style building, which was meant less to be seen as a whole than to be walked round, the design recomposing itself from different points of view.

At Windyhill, harling had suggested Scottishness as well as abstraction. In a German magazine, it might have suggested the rendered brickwork of Bavaria; but it was probably read simply as abstraction, a house without roots. This suited the modernist and mildly international assumptions of the competition. Though the second prize went to Baillie Scott, who could never have designed a house that did not look in some way English and domestic, it was precisely the fairy-tale Englishness of his exteriors which lost him the first prize. The judges admired his interiors and handling of space, but thought his exteriors not modern enough. If the Mackintoshes had not messed things up by failing to send in the interior perspectives, they would surely have won.

The house was not remarkable spatially. The Mackintoshes concentrated on the decoration of the interior, which was Koch's special interest (he was also a wallpaper manufacturer). They submitted six elevations and three perspectives. The perspective of the drawing room-cum-music room is the most ornate, and leaves you wondering whether more is not less in these Mackintosh interiors. But it has an interesting feature in the tapering posts which run along either side of the room and seem to touch the ceiling. These recall the symbolic posts at Glasgow School of Art and those which flanked the exhibit in Vienna; they make a room inside a room. We have seen hints of this before, and will see more.

After the scramble of the Art-Lover's House, Mackintosh turned to the furniture and interiors for Windyhill. William Davidson loved art but he also liked, it seems, a simple homeliness verging on austerity. The hall was a long, rectangular room to which Mackintosh applied a scheme of austere contrast: a ceiling of dark, closely-spaced joists, white walls, and a dark frieze rail, uprights and skirting boards, creating frames which also embraced the doors and windows. At the fireplace, a plain rectangular surround and a pair of tapering posts carrying their own cornice introduced a variation on the framework theme. It was all calm and rectilinear, like an interior in a 17th-century Dutch painting. The hall furniture was in the sturdy plank style, and the Davidsons would eat in here when they had family gatherings. One imagines Mr and Mrs Davidson sitting at either end of the table, in the strange high-backed chairs. The seat on these chairs spreads out towards the front, like traditional Scottish 'caqueteuse' chairs; but the back is one of Mackintosh's least traditional forms, concave, tapering, tilted backwards, and mysteriously pierced with a vesica shape near the bottom. It is an impractical design, for the back scrapes against the floor when the chair is moved; but it is also unusually well made, the concave back skilfully jointed from three pieces of well-chosen timber.

Davidson did not need new furniture throughout, and Mackintosh designed only a few pieces for the drawing room, including the

64,65

27
63

70

69

84

69 Hall chair from Windyhill,
Houston Street, Kilmacolm,
Renfrewshire, 1901. Oak, stained dark.

70 Windyhill. The hall, 1900–1901.

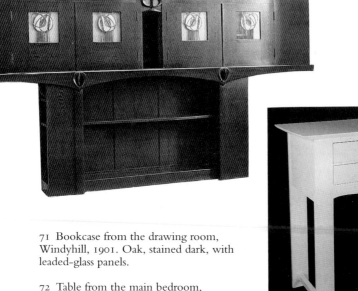

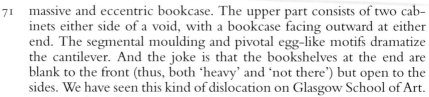

71 Bookcase from the drawing room, Windyhill, 1901. Oak, stained dark, with leaded-glass panels.

72 Table from the main bedroom, Windyhill, 1901. Oak, painted white.

71   massive and eccentric bookcase. The upper part consists of two cabinets either side of a void, with a bookcase facing outward at either end. The segmental moulding and pivotal egg-like motifs dramatize the cantilever. And the joke is that the bookshelves at the end are blank to the front (thus, both 'heavy' and 'not there') but open to the sides. We have seen this kind of dislocation on Glasgow School of Art.

72   A simple, white-painted table from the main bedroom demonstrates the games of direction Mackintosh could play with the plank style. He used planks about half an inch thick instead of ordinary legs, making the legs and carcase into a single plane. The side view seems like a different table. It was a simple trick, but the dislocation was real. Davidson might read the plank style as simple and honest; but for his architect it was wit and contradiction. In the rest of the bedroom,

65   Mackintosh used a design from the Art-Lover's House for the northwest wall, set the bed into a barrel-vaulted recess, and stencilled the walls with abstract-organic motifs. This was the bower-like setting first seen at Mains Street, and the only room at Windyhill that brings Margaret or sensuality to mind.

86

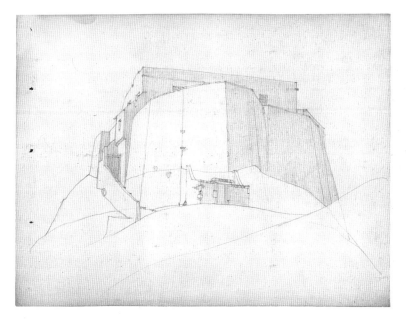

73 The Castle, Holy Island, Northumberland, July 1901. Pencil.

That summer, the Mackintoshes went to Holy Island, off the Northumberland coast, with the McNairs and Charles Macdonald, Margaret and Frances's brother. Mackintosh's sketches of flowers and buildings which survive show that he was now more than a typical Free Style draughtsman. He was skilled enough in perspective to capture the great, blank masses of the castle with the minimum of line. **73**

Mackintosh's next building was also massive and set on a hill. The **74,75** competition for an Anglican cathedral in Liverpool was announced in September 1901, with a deadline later extended to 30 June 1902. It was an open competition, in two stages, and attracted a lot of critical attention. J. F. Bentley's neo-Byzantine Westminster Cathedral had just been completed to great acclaim. Could Liverpool outdo the Catholics? And should they do it in Gothic? The Liverpool committee wanted Gothic as a requirement but were cried down by the architectural profession. Like most of the competitors including the winner, Mackintosh chose to design in Gothic anyway, taking his arrangement of crossing tower and two lesser towers at the west end from Durham Cathedral. Much of his detail, on the other hand, was

87

inspired by the church work of English Free Style architects, especially Sedding's Holy Trinity, Sloane Street, Henry Wilson's 1893 design for a cathedral in Victoria, British Columbia, and W. H. Bidlake's recently completed St Agatha's Church, Birmingham.

The assessors were Norman Shaw and G. F. Bodley, two of the architects Mackintosh had held up to admiration in his 1893 lecture. They did not select his scheme for the second stage of the competition, probably because of his implausible buttress details. Above aisle level, the nave buttresses were open at the top like flying buttresses, and solid lower down, like fins, with a frieze of figure sculpture in between. As Thomas Howarth has pointed out, they would have put an immense weight on the aisles, and deprived the clerestorey windows of light.[17] The friezes compounded this eccentricity: Mackintosh seems to have proposed that they should be carved on wedge-like blocks slung between the front edge of the buttresses and the window embrasures. In elevation they look like Margaret's dreaming ladies alternating with Mackintosh's graphic tracery, which makes a kind of sense. In perspective they look incongruous, and would have been so in reality.

The Liverpool Cathedral drawings were signed by Honeyman, Keppie and Mackintosh, for Mackintosh became a partner in the firm in 1901. He could not afford to buy a partnership in the usual way, so he was allowed to buy his way in gradually. This promotion was well deserved. It fitted his new status as a married man. And his architectural work would now be recognized as his own. But for some years now, he had thought of himself as an artist, not a professional man. A lecture of about this date, entitled 'Seemliness', was shot through with that exalted sense. Emboldened by Margaret perhaps, he spoke of art and life, and the struggle between 'the advocates of individuality, freedom of thought and personal expression on the one hand and the advocates of tradition and authority on the other'.[18] At one point his notes break into staccato as he urged his audience to take the lonely path: 'But you must be independant – independant independant, dont talk so much. . . . Shake off all the props – the props tradition and authority offer you – and go alone crawl – stumble – stagger – but go alone.'[19] This sounds autobiographical. Mackintosh was a policeman's son in an increasingly middle-class profession, and he had experienced rebuffs. His ideas of freedom versus authority and the struggle of the artist were simplistic, but he needed them to give himself strength.

At about the same time Mackintosh squashed his belief in freedom 76 and experiment into a neat square for publication in a Viennese book

Competition design for the Anglican Cathedral, Liverpool, 1901–2

74 Perspective from the south-west. Pen and ink and wash.

75 Detail of the south elevation, showing the sculptural frieze and tracery. Pen and ink and wash.

on artistic lettering: the words are a quotation from J. D. Sedding. Mackintosh never designed an alphabet; he simply drew letters as titling for his drawings and for a few signs on buildings, posters and minor graphic works. His earliest distinctive letters, on the Italian sketches for instance, were fat and stylized. The stilted, rectilinear letters with high loops and cross-strokes to A, E, F, H, P and R, and the Japanese practice of arranging his initials and other details inside a square, date from the mid-1890s and contributed to the spare, calculated elegance of his drawings and sketches for many years. 'There is hope. . .' is a formal exercise along these lines. With Mackintosh there often seems to be a battle between form and content, and here he makes letters into patterns, risking legibility. But we have a skill in recognizing letters, and can negotiate the pattern. It is more like a

76 Lettering, 1901. From Rudolf von Larisch, *Beispiele künstlerischer Schrift* (Vienna 1902).

game. Mackintosh has made a maze of letters, and we read our way out.

Late in 1901 or early in 1902, Mackintosh did some work at 14 Kingsborough Gardens, Glasgow, for Mrs Robert J. Rowat, Francis Newbery's aunt. He installed a fireplace and fitted seating in the drawing room, and decorated the walls with a stencilled pattern of loops, sprigs and roses in grey, green and mauve, which he called 'Rose Leaf'.[20] The Mackintoshes never used wallpaper, but here stencilling had some of the same effect. Stencilling was much more common in Scotland than it was in England, and Mackintosh probably studied George Walton's use of it in the Buchanan Street and Argyle Street tea rooms. But after his own first efforts at Buchanan Street, he used it quite sparingly. Stencilling would have made the Mains Street drawing room less austere, and probably much less individual. At 14 Kingsborough Gardens it introduced the more everyday luxury of delicate shades and all-over pattern. The technique of little spots of colour was not abandoned, but it lost some of its potency.

Mackintosh also designed two cabinets for Mrs Rowat's drawing room. The inside of each door was silvered, and inlaid with the figure of a woman holding an immense rose. The inlay was made of a special high-fired glass which could not be cut smoothly enough to do justice to Mackintosh's curves, and the details are consequently coarse. But Mackintosh could do anything with white-painted woodwork, and the rest of the cabinet is a three-dimensional symphony of curves: the

90

simple curve of the bracket below the lower shelf overlaid by the subtler curve of the corners of the doors, the swelling profile of the fin which slides down between the doors, the plan of the upper shelf which curves forward from the centre to the sides. This interplay cannot be photographed from a single point of view, it has to be explored. The quality of these cabinets lies in their complexity, the multitude of forms. They parade a luxury and redundancy, not of materials or workmanship, but of design.

In March 1902 *Dekorative Kunst* published the most substantial account of the Mackintoshes' work to appear during their lifetime, written by Muthesius. He took for granted that they worked together, calling them a *Künstlerpaar*, an artist-couple, and wrote more about interiors than about architecture. He began by saying that England was the birthplace of the new movement in art, but had produced nothing new since the death of William Morris in 1896. The initiative, Muthesius argued, had passed to Europe, with which the Scottish movement ran in parallel. And this initiative was associated in his mind

77 No. 14 Kingsborough Gardens, Glasgow, 1901–2. The drawing room. From Hermann Muthesius, *Das englische Haus*, vol. 3 (Berlin 1905).

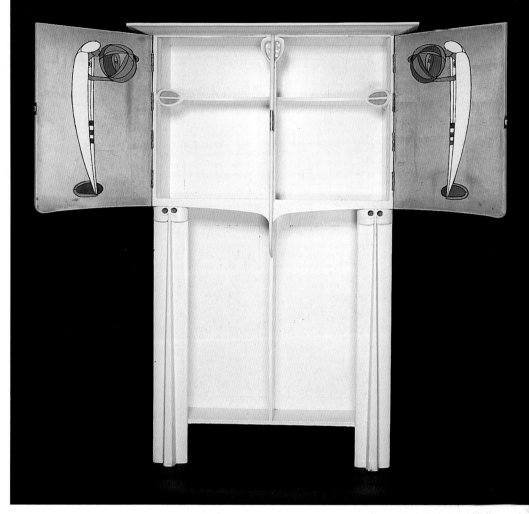

78 High-backed chair, 1902. Oak, painted white, with upholstered seat and back, the back stencilled.

79, 80 Cabinet with inlaid glass panels, 1902. Oak, painted white, the insides of the doors painted silver and inlaid with coloured glass; white metal hinges and handles. This is one of the duplicates of the Kingsborough Gardens cabinets which Mackintosh had made for the flat at 120 Mains Street.

with the room as a work of art: 'it is the room as a whole with which serious art should be concerned'.[21] He saw this idea in the work of progressive architects in Europe, and in the work of Mackintosh. But he did not see it in England, except in the work of Baillie Scott, for progressive English interiors were usually reticent, and catholic in spirit, embracing old furniture as well as new, the client's belongings as well as the architect's tastes.

The story that The Four had been ridiculed at the Arts and Crafts Exhibition in 1896 – within a few weeks of William Morris's death – suited Muthesius's thesis perfectly. Here was a British champion for the Continental phase of the new movement in art, emerging just as the leader of the old, English phase passed away. Muthesius's article stated clearly, and for the first time, that the Mackintoshes' work was greeted with protests by the English in 1896, refused admission to the Arts and Crafts Exhibition in 1899, and welcomed by the Viennese in 1900. This is the origin of a large part of the Mackintosh myth.

On the other hand, Muthesius's article contained the most perceptive contemporary account of the Mackintoshes' work. He began by saying that the Scottish character combined 'puritanism with romanticism . . . abstinence with mysticism'.[22] This national stereotype suggested a more fundamental polarity, and after the reference to Scotland the language of description divides into the austere: 'an outward austerity and sobriety of line . . . broad undecorated surfaces . . . simple boxes . . . uniform surface . . . taut sinuousness . . . puritan severity . . . severe and stiff . . . simple, almost primitive'; and the decorated: 'mysterious effects . . . special gem-like effects . . . decorative elements of supreme delicacy . . . soulful depth . . . nervous delicacy of feeling . . . a dreamy fanciful line'. It did not take much to bring the 'austere' Mackintosh and the 'decorative' Margaret together at the end of the article: 'the meaning of this opposition is fulfilment. The male and female element seem to marry.'[23] These gender stereotypes are crude; but they helped Muthesius to a fuller understanding of the furniture and interiors than any other contemporary writer.

81 The article included sketch designs for two studio-houses not seen before, one apparently in the country and the other in the town. Like the Art-Lover's House, they are easier to appreciate as drawings than as proposals for building. Mackintosh's ability to reduce mass, ornament and glazing patterns to the single medium of line makes them little graphic masterpieces. But no building, and especially no harled building, could achieve so crisp and tense an outline. Muthesius

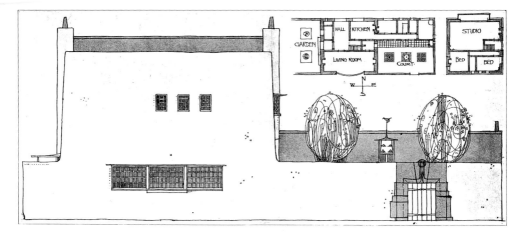

81 Design for an artist's house in the country, *c.* 1901. From *Dekorative Kunst*, vol. 9, 1902.

commented perceptively that the surfaces were so unstructured that they were 'almost ghostly'.[24] And perhaps whiteness and harling had a place in the game of absence and insubstantiality which Mackintosh was beginning to play.

In the summer of 1902 the Italian government held an International Exhibition of Modern Decorative Art in Turin. The Mackintoshes' principal exhibit, which was part of a larger Scottish section organized by Francis Newbery, was a very feminine room-setting in white, pink, silver and green. It was like their Vienna exhibit except that it was called 'The Rose Boudoir' and had roses everywhere, particularly two large gesso panels by Margaret called *Heart of the Rose* and *The White Rose and the Red Rose*. This image was at the core of the Mackintoshes' work, and reached its fullest development at Turin. In Margaret's work it seems to embody an opposition, rather like that between fertility and virginity in traditional rose-symbolism. It is warm and containing, an image of centrality, depth and renewal, but at the same time remote and impenetrable, recalling Yeats's incantatory line 'Far-off, most secret and inviolate rose'. Mackintosh's roses, if they can be distinguished as his, are more stylized, and do not seem to operate at the same symbolic level as Margaret's. David Brett has aptly described them as 'enmeshed curves that relate more to one another than to any real flower'.[25]

83

82

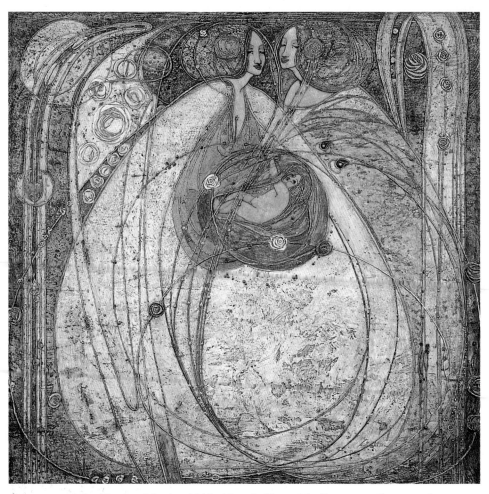

82 Margaret Macdonald Mackintosh: *Heart of the Rose*, 1902. Gesso panel.

The new furniture exhibited at Turin included two light, white-painted armchairs and an oval table, variants of designs for 14 Kingsborough Gardens, and two high-backed chairs. The white high-backed chair, now in the reconstructed Mackintosh interiors in Glasgow, shows the Mackintoshes' chairs, like the rest of their furniture and interiors, becoming lighter, more luxurious, more symbolic and perhaps more feminine. It is more delicate than the chairs for Argyle Street and Windyhill which we have already seen, and looks

80

40,69

96

less convincing in construction. The proportions are more mannered – this was the highest chair Mackintosh designed apart from a crazy thing of 1909 that stood about 6 feet (1.8 metres) tall – and though the seat is no nearer the ground than on the Kingsborough Gardens chairs, it seems so. The back is upholstered and stencilled, bringing it into line with the new wall schemes; and it is crowned by an organic and symbolic-seeming moulding. The position of this moulding, floating behind the sitter's head, helps us to understand why some of Mackintosh's chairs have been seen as ghosts or creatures, staring at us. The chair acts as a kind of cradle or reinforcement for the sitter. It is not exactly that these chairs are like people; but they are in a state of preparedness, waiting for people to sit in them. Until then, they are like ghosts.

The quiet, spare enclosure of the Mackintoshes' exhibit was in striking contrast to the bustle of the rest of the exhibition and, according to *The Studio*, added 'to the already rapidly-growing reputation of Mr. Mackintosh'.[26] In the 1940s, the German painter Friedrich Ahlers-Hestermann, who would have been an impressionable nineteen-year-old in 1902, recalled this, and perhaps other exhibits:

83 'The Rose Boudoir', part of the Mackintoshes' exhibit at the International Exhibition of Modern Decorative Art in Turin, 1902. From *Deutsche Kunst und Dekoration*, vol. 10, 1902.

84 Margaret Macdonald Mackintosh:
gesso panels from the music-room
frieze at Carl-Ludwigstrasse 45,
Vienna, 1906.

85 The music room at Carl–
Ludwigstrasse 45 in about 1903.

Here we found the strangest mixture of puritanically severe functional forms and lyrical sublimation of the practical. These rooms
were like dreams: everywhere there are small panels, grey silks, the
slenderest vertical shafts of wood, small rectangular sideboards with
upper edges that jut out, so smooth that their different parts merge
into one, so straightforward that they look as innocent and serious
as young girls about to receive Holy Communion – and altogether
unreal. . . . The fascination that these proportions exerted, and the

aristocratically spontaneous certainty with which a piece of enamel or stained glass or wrought iron was placed, enchanted all artists. . . . Here were mysticism and aestheticism, although far removed from the Christian sense of the former word, and with a strong scent of heliotrope, and a feel of well-cared-for hands, and of delicate sensuality. As if in contrast to the exuberance of what had gone before there was scarcely anything in these rooms except two upright chairs, with backs as tall as a man, which stood on a white carpet, looking at each other over a slender table, silently, like ghosts.[27]

The Mackintoshes also exhibited a sleek black writing cabinet at Turin, inset with gesso panels entitled *The Dreaming Rose* and *The Awakened Rose*. It was bought by Fritz Wärndorfer, a wealthy Viennese businessman and keen supporter of the Secession and the Wiener Werkstätte. At some time between the Vienna and Turin exhibitions, Wärndorfer had asked Mackintosh to furnish a music room in his house, Carl-Ludwigstrasse 45 (now Weimarstrasse 59) in the suburb of Wahring; Hoffmann was to remodel the dining room. Mackintosh's design dates from the spring of 1902. Work began in the summer, and it was almost complete by the end of the year.

The room was roughly 20 by 20 feet (6 by 6 metres). Mackintosh 85 panelled it in white-painted wood up to a frieze rail, designed an inglenook round the fireplace, and more fitted seating by a window, and furnished it with duplicates or variants of pieces designed for Kingsborough Gardens or Turin. At the beginning of 1903 visitors would have seen an elaborate and harmonious white Mackintosh interior, typical of its date. But there was more to come. A grand piano arrived in 1903, roughly square in plan. One expects odd-shaped furniture from Mackintosh, but in fact boxy cases were a feature of artistic pianos in Britain from at least the mid-1890s, and Mackintosh or Wärndorfer may have seen 'square' grand pianos designed by C. R. Ashbee: one was illustrated in the Viennese magazine *Kunst und Kunsthandwerk* in 1902.[28] Mackintosh's design was lightly clad in abstract-organic mouldings. And at the keyboard end were two small gesso panels by Margaret, called *The Opera of the Winds* and *The Opera of the Sea*. Much larger gesso panels by Margaret on the theme of Maeterlinck's play *Les Sept Princesses*, filling the frieze around the room, were installed in about 1907–8.

The room seems to have been celebrated among the cultured and liberal *haute bourgeoisie* who were the chief supporters of the Secession, and Ludwig Hevesi called it 'a place of spiritual joy'.[29] A music room was the perfect vehicle for the Mackintoshes' intense vision of artistic living. This one came at a high point in their collaboration, and was handled on a generous scale: they seem to have designed all the furniture and decorations. If it had survived it would be counted as their principal contribution to the room as a work of art, a concept dearer to Viennese than to British designers. To *The Studio*'s Vienna correspondent its coherence suggested music: 'The composition forms an organic whole, each part fitting into the rest with the same concord as do the passages of a grand symphony.'[30] However, Wärndorfer, bankrupted by the demands of the Wiener Werkstätte, left for the United States in 1914. The house was sold in 1916 and the interiors were either destroyed or dispersed. Only the gesso panels, large and small, are known to survive.

Mackintosh was particularly busy in 1902. While he and Margaret were working on the Wärndorfer music room, he was also working on a new house. Early in 1902 Walter Blackie, a Glasgow publisher, bought a building plot in Helensburgh, a small town beside the Firth of Clyde; he was thinking of schools for his children and somewhere to sail his yacht. Talwin Morris was the Art Manager at Blackie & Son and he recommended Mackintosh as architect. At their first meeting Blackie told Mackintosh that he 'rather fancied grey rough cast for the walls, and slate for the roof; and that any architectural effect sought should be secured by the massing of the parts rather than by adventitious ornamentation'.[31] Mackintosh showed him Windyhill and the job was his.

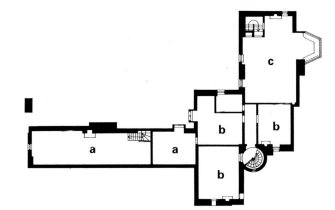

ATTIC

a box room
b bedroom
c school room

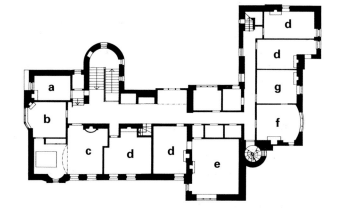

FIRST FLOOR

a bathroom
b dressing room
c principal bedroom
d bedroom
e guest bedroom
f day nursery
g night nursery

30 ft

10 m

N

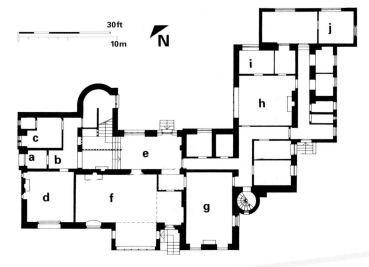

GROUND FLOOR

a porch
b vestibule
c cloakroom
d library
e hall
f drawing room
g dining room
h kitchen
i scullery
j laundry

86 The Hill House, Upper Colquhoun Street, Helensburgh, Dunbartonshire, 1902–4, Plans of the ground, first and attic floors, The plan of the ground floor is based on survey drawings of the building in 1974, with amendments.

87, 88 The Hill House.
Entrance, and view from the
south-east.

Today, as you walk up the slope on which Helensburgh stands, you pass grey stone villas of the 1860s, and then bigger houses with Scottish Baronial roofscapes, or warm red tiles and timber-framing in the English manner. These were the houses of Glasgow businessmen, built since the railway arrived in 1857, and they are arranged in a grid of neat, suburban plots. At the top, you come to a house that is harled all over, striking in its pale simplicity. This is Walter Blackie's The Hill House.

86,49   The plan followed that of Windyhill, with a roughly rectangular hall and the principal rooms ranged along the south front, looking out towards the Clyde. But it was a much bigger house, costing just under £6,000 compared to Windyhill's £2,500. When it was finished in 1904, Mackintosh said to Blackie: 'Here is the house. It is not an Italian Villa, an English Mansion House, a Swiss Chalet, or a Scotch Castle. It is a Dwelling House.'[32] Like many serious-minded Free Style architects, he presented his work as styleless. Blackie took much the same view: 'the freshness or newness of Mackintosh's productions sprang from his striving to serve the practical needs of the occupants.'[33]

We cannot doubt this kind of experience, and Blackie enjoyed The Hill House for the rest of his life. But even a superficial inspection will show that more things than practicality were involved.

In Scottish gentry houses of the 16th and 17th centuries, and in the turn-of-the-century houses modelled on them, it was common for elaborate carving to grace the stonework of the entrance. The entrance in the narrow west front of The Hill House is, by compari- 87 son, brutally understated. It is not easy to understand what Mackintosh was doing here. Perhaps he was expressing an unusual and difficult sense of the relationship between outside and inside. The massive architrave suggests the thickness of the sandstone walls under the harling. This entrance does not offer a welcome or a place of transition. It is a boundary. You must penetrate the thickness of the walls in order to move from one world to another.

From the south-east the three different parts of Mackintosh's 88 design are obvious. The two-storey range contains most of the family rooms. The three-storey cross-wing contains the dining room, guest bedroom and an attic bedroom. And a parallel three-storey range,

89 The Hill House. The service wing seen from the north-east.

pivoted around a very Scottish stair tower, contains the service wing and children's rooms. Confusingly, the ascent in size reverses the social hierarchy of the house. The family range with its cross-wing was modelled on James Maclaren's Glenlyon Farmhouse of 1889–90, and has a more sheltered terrace than Windyhill. But the windows are arranged with the same careful asymmetry as at Windyhill and, with almost nothing else on these walls to look at, we begin to notice how much the windows vary in size, depth of reveal, type (sash, casement, fixed), materials (wood, iron, lead) and glazing patterns. We also notice how the library window at the west end has a particularly deep reveal, over which the wall swells out in a segmental curve pierced by a tiny window, like a Scottish tower sliced off above and below. And, as if this were not puzzling enough, the tiny window is flanked by mysterious blocks. (These may have been destined for carving, but in their harled state they look more like petrified shutters.)

The gable of the dining-room wing appears difficult and abstract at first, but it is rich in meanings. It is a game of directions, with gable, chimneystack and massive, rectangular dormer pitted against each other, and the dormer turned through ninety degrees. It is materials, and the paradox that Mackintosh could make a skin of harling express the layered thickness of the walls. It is history, and the paradox that Crathes Castle may have been the exemplar for this and other details 7 on the house, and yet this is the most abstract, proto-Modern feature of Mackintosh's work that we have seen so far. And finally it is proof, if proof be needed, that the newness of Mackintosh's work did not always spring from his striving to serve the practical needs of the occupants, for all this complexity has nothing whatever to do with the simple attic bedroom behind it.

The service wing seen from the north-east presents several elements 89 nested around each other, as at Windyhill. The composition is not taut, like the principal fronts, but neither is it careless. It is unambitious, additive building in a place that will not attract attention, and

90 The Hill House. The north front.

90   it is often overlooked. The north front, on the other hand, was a more
presented part, and Mackintosh drew it in one of his mannered per-
91   spectives, including the unexecuted billiard room. Quite apart from
the billiard room, drawing and reality are far apart. In reality, this side
of the house feels as if it is paying the price of studied compositions
on other fronts. The tangle of down-pipes is not a trivial sign of this,
for Mackintosh had used a down-pipe to excellent effect on the east
wing of Glasgow School of Art. But there was too much for him to
sort out at the back of The Hill House.

Having walked around the building we will not go in, for the interiors and furniture belong to a later date; but we should not leave
without taking note of Mackintosh's windows. It turns out that The
Hill House has fifty-eight windows to about forty different designs.
The size of reveals remains fairly constant, but the square or rectangle
of the pane is constantly altered. This is not new in Mackintosh's
work, though it may be extreme. Convenience, propriety and the
Scottish tradition all required variety of windows, but not forty in a
total of fifty-eight. Mackintosh's increasing fascination with the square
was at work, as his perspective shows. Glazing bars were his delight,
and he must design new patterns for almost every window.

We should not look for a coherent whole at The Hill House.
Mackintosh started from a permissive, Free Style position, and added
his own extraordinary appetite for new and various forms. (All-over
harling makes it look simple and draws the design together, but it is
only a skin over various masses.) The result is not the radical discontinuity of Glasgow School of Art, but a genial looseness such as

106

we have already seen in the Art-Lover's House, where the design re-assembles itself from different points of view.

The Hill House was a long time building. The roof was on by January 1903, but it was not complete until about a year later. During much of 1903 the Mackintoshes were working on new tea rooms in Sauchiehall Street, Glasgow's most up-to-the-minute shopping street. The job involved recasting 217 Sauchichall Street for Miss Cranston, the tenant, and refurbishing the next-door building for the ground landlord.[34] Mackintosh virtually rebuilt the street front of 217. He set 92 the ground floor back from the street and glazed it with small panes as George Walton had done at Argyle Street, so that it looked discreet but welcoming, not like a plate-glass shop front. Above, he translated the existing mid-Victorian stuccoed front into the language of The

91 The Hill House. Perspective from the north-west, 1903. Pen and ink. From *Deutsche Kunst und Dekoration*, vol. 15, 1905.

92 The Willow Tea Rooms, 217 Sauchiehall Street, Glasgow, 1903. The street front.

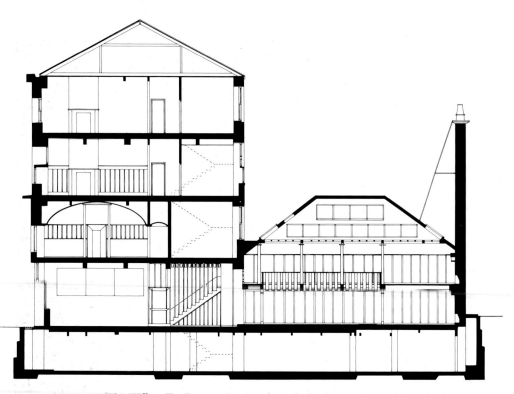

93 The Willow Tea Rooms. Section through the depth of the building, looking east.

Hill House, stripping away the mouldings and substituting two simple cornices. He designed a shallow bow to the first floor which, over the ground-floor void, reminds us of the slice of tower at The Hill House, and a two-storey bow above which is pure form unrelated to the plan. He punched windows deep in the wall, and ran strips of Viennese squares up the sides, under the cornice, and into the reveals.[35] What was he doing? This was a showy city building, but instead of his beloved mouldings he used simple stucco curves and squares. It was as if he had learned, after working on Windyhill and The Hill House, that the geometry of the harled Scottish vernacular, removed from its domestic context, was still geometry.

At 217 Sauchiehall Street the structural shell was already there. All Mackintosh had to do was define the spaces and play games with space.[36] The section shows four storeys and basement at the front and an extension of one storey and basement at the back. Mackintosh arranged three tea rooms on the ground floor (one at the front, one

88

93

108

94 The Willow Tea Rooms. The front tea room, looking towards the lunch room and tea gallery at the back of the building

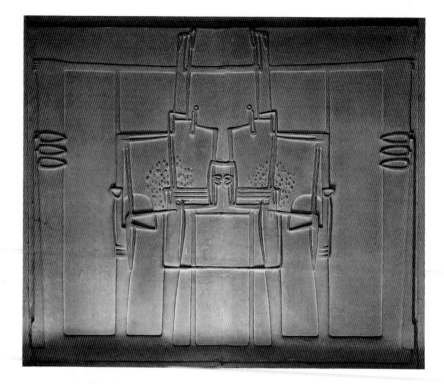

at the back, and one in the gallery), an exclusive vaulted room on the first floor, and billiard and smoking rooms on the second. The extension was top-lit with a wide central well, and where it butted up against the front building there was a gap of about 3 feet (90 centimetres) between the floor of the gallery and the ceiling of the front room. Mackintosh filled this gap with a light metal screen, and designed another screen of thin metal rods for the stairs. The view from the front room towards the extension shows how the screens and the gallery created distinct spaces, while light and vision could pass through them. One of the pleasures of eating at Miss Cranston's was watching other people.

Sauchiehall means 'alley of willows' and No. 217 was called The Willow Tea Rooms. Willow motifs recurred throughout, but the character of the abstract-organic decorations derived less from nature than from strong angular curves, as if the curves were fighting against squares and the squares were beginning to win. The front room was decorated with a scheme of white, silver and rose appropriate to a ladies' tea room, but some of the fittings would be extraordinary in any context. In the centre was a strange, unnameable structure framing two tables, the purest and least structural example of the wooden fantasies with which Mackintosh liked to define space. And the frieze was filled, not with dreaming women as at Ingram Street, but with an almost abstract pattern on repeated plaster panels. It was called *The Willow Tree* but its tense, branch-like forms suggest a recti-linear geometry, or perhaps the shape of a man, more than an ordi-nary willow. It has the staring quality of Epstein's *Rock Drill*, and here for once historians are right to speak of Mackintosh as anticipating the Moderns. 95

The back room, which was a lunch room for men and women, was panelled in dark oak and grey canvas, and hung with textile panels of women – or rather of women's heads surrounded by roses, their bodies reduced to irregular rectangles. The gallery was not supported by columns, but by four massive steel joists which kept this sombre space clear. The tea gallery above was fitted out as a rose-bower in pink, white and grey; and here there were columns, a little forest of symbolic trees, resting on the joists below and supporting an almost weightless ceiling above. 96 97

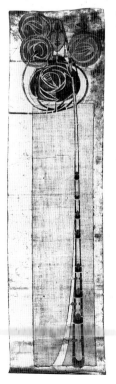

95 *The Willow Tree*, a plaster panel designed for the Willow Tea Rooms, 1903. This example was installed in the Mackintoshes' house, 6 Florentine Terrace.

96 The Willow Tea Rooms. Textile panel in the lunch room.

97 The Willow Tea Rooms. The tea gallery.

98 The Salon de Luxe.

99 The doors to the Salon de Luxe.

Set apart from these spaces on the first floor, white, intimate, and
98 lined with mirrors, was the Salon de Luxe. (Or 'the Room de Looks'
as the Glasgow journalist Neil Munro dubbed it.)[37] The dado was
upholstered in silk, and panels of leaded mirror-glass ran round the
walls, enlarging the room and reflecting the customers' self-esteem.
On one side was the fireplace, on the other a gesso panel of enmeshed
women by Margaret called *O ye, all ye who walk in Willowwood*, which
is the first line of a sad sonnet by Rossetti. The leaded glass reached a
99 climax in the magnificent double doors filled with stalks, buds, roseballs and the streaming, looping lines of Margaret's paintings. The
chandelier was a cascade of coloured glass balls, and under it, around
the central tables, were high-backed chairs painted silver and upholstered in purple velvet, creating an inner circle (no, an inner square)
of exclusiveness. The Salon de Luxe was a room chiefly for ladies, and
it was one culmination of the series of collaborative interiors which
began at Mains Street. It was not as personal as Mains Street, or as thematic as The Rose Boudoir, or as serious as Warndorfer's music room,
But it expressed more intensely than any of these the luxury of design
– even the waitresses wore dresses and chokers designed by
Mackintosh. Three years before, the Mackintoshes' version of art-
and-domesticity at Ingram Street had been too subjective, too tentative; in the lower rooms at the Willow it could seem angular and
difficult. But in the Salon de Luxe they made the overstatement that
a place of public refreshment needs. This was the commercial version
of the room as a work of art.

The Willow was opened on 29 October 1903 and was greeted with
enthusiasm in the local press: 'until the opening of Miss Cranston's
new establishment in Sauchiehall Street today, the acme of originality had not been reached' . . . 'Her "Salon de Luxe" on the first floor
is simply a marvel of the art of the upholsterer and decorator.'[38] The
Mackintoshes had created a chic interior that was startlingly novel,
easy to appreciate, and open to the public. They could not have advertised themselves, or Miss Cranston, better.

While the Willow was being fitted out, Mackintosh was asked to
design a new Board School in Scotland Street, just south of the Clyde.
The main lines of the design were settled by the end of 1903, though
100 the building was not completed until July 1906. The plan follows a
standard Glasgow School Board type, with separate, matching
entrances and staircases for boys and girls, and classrooms off a central
101 corridor. The entrance front is boldly modelled, symmetrical and
clearly articulated: classrooms in the centre, with a cornice marking

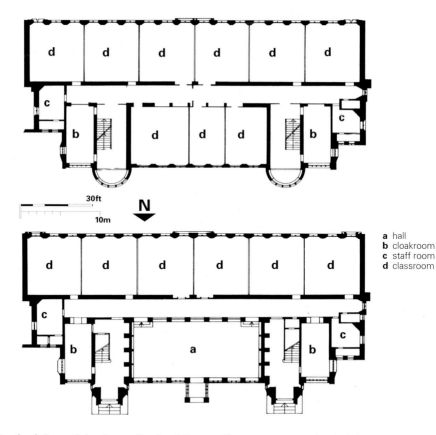

30ft
10m

N

a hall
b cloakroom
c staff room
d classroom

100, 101 Scotland Street School, 255 Scotland Street, Glasgow, 1903–6. Plans of the ground and first floors (*above* and *top*), and entrance front.

Scotland Street School

102 A stair landing, looking towards the curved window bay.

103 The entrance front from the north-west.

off the second floor as an attic in the Classical manner, then stair towers, then cloakrooms arranged as mezzanines, then teachers' rooms. But, since this was Mackintosh, there were games afoot. The stair towers were modelled on traditional Scottish towers which have a spiral stair, thick walls and a few small windows – but Mackintosh substituted walls of glass. This is the game of solid and void. And, as the plan shows, the stairs are not spirals: they have straight flights, and landings which look out into semi-circular wells of light. This is the gap between outside and in. The disposition of these towers antici-pates that of the glass-clad stairs on Walter Gropius's famous Werkbund factory of 1914. But Gropius's stairs were a true spiral, his towers a rational exercise in transparency and truth.

The back of the building was flat, a uniform range of eighteen classroom windows. Mackintosh framed the two central and the two outermost windows with delicate tracery, creating the ghostly pres-ence of a centrepiece and wings, as on a Classical building. There is perhaps a game of ambiguity here. The front of the building is more elaborate, but it is almost as if Mackintosh wished to suggest, in the

Scotland Street School

104 The rear elevation.

105 Thistle and Tree of Life motifs on the rear elevation.

flat formality of the back of the school, the sense of a front, while the additive massing of his front feels like a back.

The detailing, which may date from as late as mid-1905, is typically playful and original, but it articulates the building more effectively than Mackintosh had ever done before. He used his mannered and complex architraves to tie the cubic forms of the entrances into the cylinders of the towers. He made the infants' entrance in the centre tenderly small, and shortened the architraves on the other entrances from their Classical norms. He gave the stonework round the top of the main tower-windows movement and life with little peaked or winged motifs, and marked the transition to the topmost range of windows with a band of vertical mouldings on which the winged motif is disposed like notes on a musical stave. We have seen at Mains Street how Mackintosh's organic ornament had a vital quality. So it is here. After several years with the harled Scottish vernacular, which has few mouldings and moves from wall to window, solid to void, in an instant, Mackintosh returned to stone and a public building, and created mouldings which give life to the stone and make a transition between wall and window. At the back, the stylized central images are a Scottish thistle and a Tree of Life, composed of Viennese-inspired squares and triangles.[39]

Scotland Street stands apart from most of Mackintosh's other buildings. It is symmetrical. It uses Classical methods of articulation. Its interior is plain and straightforward. Above all it is a coherent whole, without looseness or discontinuity. Much of the appeal of the building lies in its clarity, which Mackintosh's games do not disturb. The role of the client is important here. The School Board presented Mackintosh with a standard plan, a limited purse, and a clear idea of what they wanted. And there were clashes, as we shall see. But Mackintosh would often give of his best when he had something to fight against.

At this point we must return to The Hill House, for the interior belongs to the end of 1903 and the beginning of 1904. This was the Mackintoshes' most elaborate domestic interior, the nearest they came to a real Art-Lover's House; but it was not comprehensive. It

106 The Hill House, Helensburgh. The library, 1903–4.

seems that Blackie could not afford to decorate and furnish the whole house to their designs so, though their inimitable detailing runs throughout, their efforts were concentrated on the library, hall, drawing room and principal bedroom.

107
106 Through a black door pierced with squares, we enter a low vestibule. On the right is the library, panelled in dark wood inlaid in places with squares of coloured glass. It is masculine, sober and almost completely rectilinear, but here and there a tall, tapering moulding sweeps up in a shallow curve across the face of the squares, as if to

107 contradict them. From the vestibule, we go up four steps into the hall, which is articulated with dark, rectilinear framing, like Windyhill, only this is the luxurious version: the broad uprights are inlaid with pale purple enamelled glass and the space between is stencilled with abstract-organic motifs as angular as those at the Willow Tea Rooms in blue, pink, purple and green.

108, 109 From the hall we move to the drawing room, and from half-light into light. The walls were painted white and decorated with stencilled roseballs and trellis patterns in pink, green and grey and with strips of

107 The Hill House. The hall looking towards the vestibule, 1903–4.

The Hill House. The drawing room, 1903–4

108 The window bay. The original decoration had been painted over, and the scheme seen here belongs to a restoration of the early 1980s; a new restoration is planned. The easy chair in the foreground was designed for the house by Mackintosh in 1905.

109 The fireplace. The frame above the mantelshelf was later filled with a gesso panel by Margaret Macdonald Mackintosh. On the right, one of Walter Blackie's 'ordinary' pieces of furniture sits uneasily in the exclusive Mackintosh setting.

silver paper. At first, the focus of the room is unclear: there is a piano in a low-ceilinged bay on the left, a window-seat in a broad, light-filled bay in front of us, and a fireplace tucked away in a corner. But it turns out that Mackintosh designed the room to work three ways: as a place for music, a place for sitting in the sun, and a warm place in winter (which he made snug with a big couch and a box-like chair like that at Mains Street). The squares on the carpet in the middle suggest the alternative arrangements.

The stairs begin in a cage of uprights, the framing of the hall worked up into one of Mackintosh's wooden fantasies, and then turn to the right, rising at an almost stately pace through the gracious, light-filled space of the apsidal tower. They bring us to the principal bedroom. The light is often soft in here. The white bed sits in a barrel-vaulted recess, its head hung originally with embroidered panels of dreaming women. A delicate hedge of stencilled roses in olive green and pink fading to grey runs round the cream-coloured walls. The creamy-white furniture is either fitted or placed with exquisite care. Here we have reached some kind of furthest point, where we can ask what veiled exotic, what long-haired Maeterlinckian princess will lie on these white sheets. (Or, what was Mrs Blackie like?)

The Hill House bedroom is a worthy successor to that at Mains Street – less intense, but larger and more luxurious. It includes, however, amongst the furniture, two light and intensely mannered ladderback chairs which could never have been designed for Mains Street, for they are black. (People are struck by the flimsiness of these

112

57

110

110 Ladderback chair in the principal bedroom of The Hill House, 1903. Ebonized oak.

111 The Hill House. Stencilled chequerboard pattern in the porch, 1903–4.

chairs, but they were probably only meant for laying clothes on.) We have seen black furniture before, but not in the heart of the feminine domain. Something was coming to an end.

The Hill House is not just a sequence of rooms: it is a home whose largest meanings and smallest details were transformed by the Mackintoshes' art. The transformation involved a loss of robustness and ordinariness, and a gain in serene, controlled and expressive spaces, full of the luxury of design. As we move around the house, we find it full of alternations and gradations of light which reinforce the masculine/feminine scheme of meanings: gloom in the vestibule, half-light in the hall, bright light beckoning us on the stairs and welcoming us in the drawing room and bedroom. Coloured light comes from squares of glass inset in doors and free-standing uprights, purple and blue in the masculine domains, pink and white in the feminine. When the sun comes out, the whole house responds to it.

The house is also full of squares: squares in fours and eights and nines, coloured squares and black-and-white chequerboards, squares on carpets telling you where to go. They are not intrusive; by now the square was less a motif in Mackintosh's hands than a method of articulating surfaces and spaces. From about 1900 one can feel it challenging the curves which characterized his mouldings of the 1890s and the organic ornament of the early 1900s. The Hill House is a point of transition. In the porch (itself a point of transition) a design is stencilled several times in black and white, a chequerboard with an 111 elegant, curving stem and bud laid upon it as a white presence, or an

123

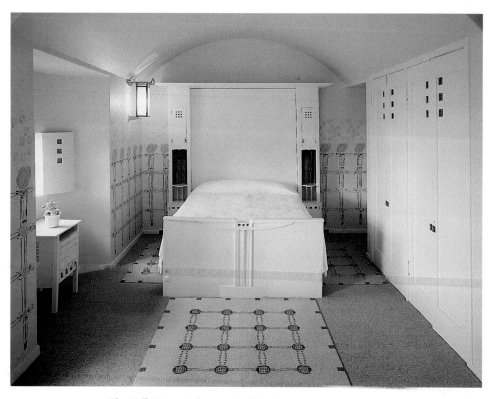

112 The Hill House. The principal bedroom, 1903–4.

absence. The principal phases of Mackintosh's decorative work seem to be implied in this simple design.

The Blackies took possession of The Hill House in the spring of 1904, when designs were being prepared for a house of almost the same name, Hous'hill. This was a mansion of 17th- and 19th-century dates on the southern outskirts of Glasgow; and in 1904 the tenants were Major John Cochrane and his redoubtable wife, Miss Catherine Cranston. Hous'hill will never have the place in Mackintosh's work that The Hill House has for it was only an interior, the furniture was dispersed in 1933, and the house was later demolished. But it had its own very different appeal. The interior was spare and intelligent, with none of the decorative intensity of The Hill House, and it fitted perfectly into the existing building.

In the dining room, a frieze rail ran round the room and across the windows, with dark walls below, and box-like light-fittings over the table. Like the drawing-room interior at Mains Street, this scheme accepted the room as it stood and was quite at home with the clients' traditional furniture and William Morris upholstery fabric. But there was one disturbing note. The walls were stencilled with a repeating pattern in two parts: below, a free and abstract composition of oblongs and irregular rectangles, above, clusters of roseballs, and tentative curves as if something was being drawn with difficulty. In the porch at The Hill House, everything seemed so tidy – curves followed by squares. Now we are faced with something new and different, and we do not know what it is. It could be a stylized vase of flowers. On the other hand the Mackintosh enthusiast Timothy Neat has suggested that it is Margaret's naked body 'mildly disguised'.[40] How he knows that it is *Margaret's* body is hard to understand. But the suggestion of a naked torso, once made, is hard to get away from. It would be surprising if Major Cochrane and his wife wanted naked women on their dining-room wall. But perhaps it was a vase of flowers to them and a naked Margaret to the designer, an extreme example of the gap between public and private meanings in Mackintosh's work.

Hous'hill, Nitshill, Glasgow, 1904–5

113 The dining room.

114 Design for stencil decorations in the dining room. Pencil.

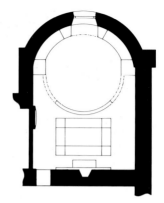

Hous'hill

115 Plan of the drawing room.

116 The drawing room.

115, 116   The drawing room was upstairs with a curved window-bay at one end, and the plan was focused on the piano, the window-bay and the hearth, as at The Hill House. Mackintosh may have seen the arrangement of curved window-bay, fitted seats and openwork screens exhibited by the Viennese architect Carl Witzmann at Turin in 1902, for at Hous'hill a curved, open screen of white-painted fins divided the room, marking out a place for the piano.[41] It was a light wooden construction subdividing space and in that sense one of Mackintosh's wooden fantasies. But in fact there was no element of fantasy in the design. It was simple, functionally effective and formally satisfying. It

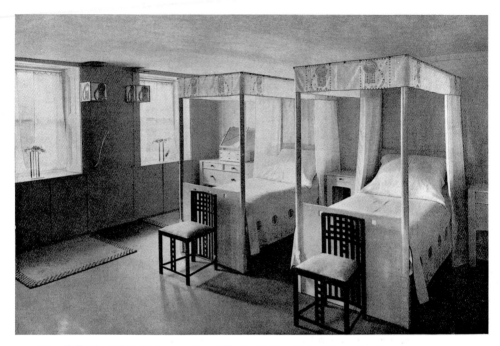

117 Hous'hill. The White Bedroom. From *The Studio Year-Book of Decorative Art 1907*.

formed a segment of a circle, answered by the window-bay; and its top rail was a complete circle, resting on the fitted seats and spanning the spaces between. The plan shows the simple relationship of this circle to the rectangle formed by the carpet in front of the fire. The chairs in front of the screen had a clear form and a stylish curve to the back, while the stretchers running along the floor perhaps owed a debt to Hoffmann and Moser.[42]

Two low-ceilinged bedrooms in the older part of the house were furnished in 1904, the Blue Bedroom which had dark-stained furniture, a definite departure from the light-feminine code, and the White Bedroom which obeyed the code but looked more like a hospital- or convent-room than a sensuous bower. This room was carefully controlled: all the carcase furniture in the photograph observed the height of the window sills; higher up, the bed valances, light fittings and delicate stencilled patterns formed a single band 9 inches (23 centimetres) deep decorated with a common motif. Such control was not new

117

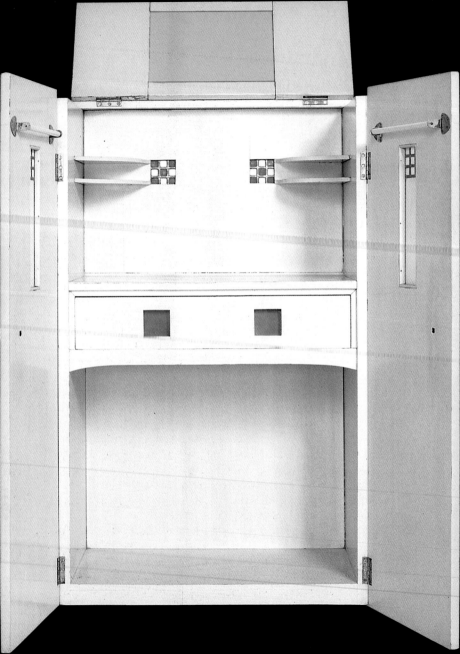

in the Mackintoshes' work. But it was combined with a drastic simplification of forms, a purging in the interests of the square. The wash-stand from this room is a box with flap-like doors; it is a radical, rectilinear design. And it is neither sensual nor complicated.

The White Bedroom was an ordinary little room, but it reveals an important change in Mackintosh's work. To understand this, we must look more closely at the central motif of his work at this date, the square. It is not the austerity of the square that matters here, but its richness, its ability to generate its own order and complexity. For Mackintosh it was a means of articulation, bringing a plain surface to life as the little spots of colour had brought the white interiors to life. It was three-dimensional, a hole as often as a mark. And it was a generative form, setting up relationships with other squares and with the spaces in between, white to their black, solid to their void. Surprisingly, it was not symbolic. The Mackintoshes' organic ornament was rich in symbolism, and Mackintosh had read W. R. Lethaby on the symbolism of the square in *Architecture, Mysticism and Myth*. But for him the square was a formal device, of great subtlety and fruitfulness, not a symbol. The more he used it, the more abstract his work became, appealing to a rational rather than a Romantic imagination.

I do not wish to argue that the square played a dominant role in the White Bedroom or in other parts of Hous'hill, rather that it implied a challenge to important themes in the collaborative interiors of 1900–1904, and that the consequences of this became clear at Hous'hill. It challenged, obviously, the curvilinear forms of organic ornament. It broke the link between designed objects and the world of nature, for the square has no associations in nature. And it offered little scope for that mixture of sensuousness and spirituality which observers, especially in Germany, felt was the strongest note in the Mackintoshes' interiors. If these things were what Margaret brought to the collaboration, then it also challenged her. In describing Hous'hill I have tried to avoid attributing the designs either to 'Mackintosh' or to 'the Mackintoshes' because I do not know what part she played. But it feels as if her share was less.

In 1904 Mackintosh and Francis Newbery stood as godfathers to Muthesius's third son, Eckart, and at Christmas Margaret wrote a chatty letter to Muthesius, giving him news of both godfathers and telling him how the School of Art was increasingly staffed by Frenchmen – Professors Delville for painting, Artôt for the Antique, Giraldon for design, and most recently Eugène Bourdon for

118 A wash-stand from the White Bedroom, Hous'hill, 1904. Wood, painted white, inlaid with panels of leaded glass and metal.

architecture. All this, Bourdon particularly, represented the growing importance at the School of a strict, academic training on the lines of the Ecole des Beaux-Arts. In an aside, Margaret wrote: 'It is very amusing – and in spite of all the efforts to stamp out the Mackintosh influence – the whole town is getting covered with imitations of Mackintosh tea rooms, Mackintosh shops Mackintosh furniture &c – It is too funny – I wonder how it will end.'[43] Then she went back to deriding Professor Giraldon. The aside suggests that she associated the Frenchmen with efforts to counter her husband's influence and assumed that Muthesius would do the same.

After Hous'hill, which was more or less complete by the end of 1904, Mackintosh probably began work on his contribution to a German exhibition of interiors which Muthesius had introduced him to. It was planned for the spring of 1905, in the Berlin showrooms of the furniture manufacturer A. S. Ball. Instead of a light, feminine interior, as at Vienna and Turin, he exhibited a dining room; the walls were dark and the furniture was made of oak stained grey green. The tables and chairs were a dark version of those for the Salon de Luxe, and the fitted furniture consisted of a sideboard, dresser and clock, all severely rectilinear. Here the square certainly did play a dominant role. The reviewer in *Kunst und Kunsthandwerk* found the dining room 'very simple, constructional, with no mysterious suggestions in the ornament'.[44] And if Mackintosh himself saw the German reviews, he would have been pleased to see details of other exhibits which showed his influence, in the dining room by Joseph Maria Olbrich and the vestibule by the Berlin architect Alfred Grenander.

This was Mackintosh's last major exhibit in Europe. So it is a good place at which to pause and consider the subject of his reputation and influence outside Britain. (Mackintosh was most involved in Europe just at the time when he was collaborating most intensely with Margaret; so here we have to think of Europeans responding sometimes to Mackintosh, sometimes to them both.) According to the Mackintosh myth, his work was acclaimed by progressive architects in Europe, received exceptional publicity in European periodicals, and influenced a generation of European architects and designers. Filippo Alison, a specialist on Mackintosh's furniture, has written that Mackintosh was 'the best known living architect in Europe' in the early 1900s.[45] A prophet, the myth reminds us, is not without honour save in his own country.

As in the case of Vienna, evidence can be marshalled to support this view. The Mackintoshes could count some of the most progressive

119

119 Dining-room interior for the A. S. Ball exhibition, Berlin, 1905. From *Deutsche Kunst und Dekoration*, vol. 16, 1905.

and influential architects in Europe among their friends and admirers. Muthesius was far and away the most important of them: he offered the Mackintoshes publicity, friendship, even a place in history. Olbrich told his bride-to-be, rather fancifully, that they should get married in Glasgow because only 'dear Mackintosh' was worthy to listen to their vows.[46] And, according to Fritz Wärndorfer, Mackintosh and Josef Hoffmann were delighted with each other.[47] There is also the slightly contextless story, told by Francis Newbery's widow Jessie, that in 1913 a gathering of architects and designers at a banquet in Breslau (now Wrocław) toasted Mackintosh as 'the greatest since the Gothic'.[48]

Knowledge of the Mackintoshes' work would have been carried beyond this circle of acquaintance by exhibitions and illustrated periodicals. We have seen their principal exhibits in Europe; they also exhibited rooms in Moscow (1902–3) and Dresden (1903–4), and

131

individual objects in Vienna (1909) and Paris (1914). About half a dozen articles appeared in British and German magazines, and the portfolio of drawings for the Art-Lover's House, if printed in any quantity, would have been an excellent advertisement.

Furthermore, there are specific examples of the Mackintoshes' influence. We have already seen some in Vienna and at the A. S. Ball exhibition. The pages of German and Austrian magazines show their influence on light fittings at an exhibition in Berlin in 1903, an office in the museum at Posen (now Poznań) by Alfred Grenander, and work by Grenander's pupils in Berlin.[49] When Peter Behrens designed a temperance restaurant at an exhibition in Düsseldorf in 1904, he gave it ladderback chairs like those for the Willow Tea Rooms. And the house which Muthesius designed for himself near Berlin in 1906 had an apsidal staircase tower, and window-seats like those at Windyhill and The Hill House.[50] These examples do not amount to much; but further research may reveal more.

Finally there is the evidence of one important contemporary observer, the polymathic Edinburgh sociologist Patrick Geddes, who was a friend and admirer of Mackintosh's. In *Cities in Evolution* (1915), Geddes wrote that 'Mackintosh' was an accepted architectural term from Belgium to Hungary, and that his influence was to be seen in city after city.[51] Geddes' comments are valuable both for what they show, and for what they fail to show. One can imagine that the Mackintoshes' work caused a stir in Vienna and Turin, and that the image of their strange, spiritual interiors acted as a yeast in European architecture and design, helping to ferment the new movement in art. Geddes seems to have heard the echoes of that. But it is interesting that when he came to give examples of the influence he claimed to have seen in city after city, he could only quote Olbrich's Tietz department store in Düsseldorf of 1906–9, a building which shows hardly any influence from Mackintosh and a great deal from the work of Alfred Messel in Berlin. For the fact is that it is not easy to find examples of European work that show the visible influence of Mackintosh. Geddes' remarks demonstrate that in Europe 'Mackintosh' was more a name to be conjured with than an example to be followed.

I do not want to suggest that Mackintosh had little or no influence in Europe, only to show that accounts of his influence have been exaggerated or unbalanced. Timothy Neat, for instance, has written of the Mackintoshes' 'pan-European success', whereas the evidence suggests that their influence was largely confined to Germany and

Austria.[52] They were known in Moscow, probably through the enthusiasm of Fedor Shekhtel who designed the remarkable 'Russian Village' at Glasgow's International Exhibition of 1901. But they do not appear to have had any special reputation or influenced specific works in Spain, Italy, Scandinavia, Holland or Belgium. There was a spirit of progressive regionalism in Eastern European countries which paralleled the spirit of some of their work, but there was little that Czech or Hungarian architects or designers could learn from their forms; one Hungarian critic found Mackintosh's work inventive but unliveable-with, and recommended that English examples should be followed.[53] In France the progressive magazine *Art et Décoration* published an article on 'Scottish Interiors' in 1907 and singled out Mackintosh for criticism, saying that compared to the funereal dining room at Mains Street, 'a chilly convent cell with bare and whitened walls would seem riotously gay'.[54] If we look further afield to the United States, an important sphere of influence for British architects and designers at this date, we find that Mackintosh's work was published only once. Some of the designs for furniture or interiors by Harvey Ellis and Charles P. Limbert show that they had seen Mackintosh's work in English and German magazines, but the sturdy and straightforward character of progressive American furniture is unlike much of Mackintosh's work.[55] The urge to link Mackintosh with Frank Lloyd Wright is irresistible to some, but there appears to be no connection between the two men or their work.[56]

Equally large claims have been made for the publicity accorded to Mackintosh. Roger Billcliffe wrote that 'Mackintosh's work and ideas were perhaps more widely disseminated than those of any architect before him.'[57] This point needs to be looked at carefully, and in context. The full list of substantial periodical articles dealing with the Mackintoshes is as follows:

1897   an introductory article by Gleeson White in *The Studio*
1898   an introductory article in *Dekorative Kunst*, possibly by Muthesius
1901   a set of illustrations in *Ver Sacrum*, and a review of the Vienna Secession exhibition in *Dekorative Kunst*, about half of which was a long quotation from Muthesius
1902   Muthesius's long article in *Dekorative Kunst*, and reviews of the Scottish exhibit at Turin in *The Studio* and *Deutsche Kunst und Dekoration* (including a long quotation from Muthesius)

1905 an article about the Willow Tea Rooms in *Dekorative Kunst*, and about The Hill House in *Deutsche Kunst und Dekoration*, both by the Mackintoshes' friend Fernando Agnoletti

To these we should add details of the *Glasgow Herald* building in Muthesius's *Die englische Baukunst der Gegenwart* (1900), the portfolio of drawings for the Art-Lover's House (1902) with an introduction by Muthesius, and the passages on Mackintosh in Muthesius's *Das englische Haus* of 1904–5.

This list shows how much the Mackintoshes' reputation depended on the advocacy of one man, and Muthesius held a very particular view. Though, like other German critics, he valued the practical and homely qualities of English architecture, he saw in the Mackintoshes artists of an extreme originality and spirituality, expressed in rough-cast houses, mystical-seeming white interiors, modelled furniture and dreaming women. Of a more robust, less aesthetic Mackintosh, he published only the *Glasgow Herald* building. It is probable that Scotland Street School was not illustrated in Germany, and that no architectural view of Glasgow School of Art appeared in print outside Glasgow before 1924.

It also shows that attention paid to the Mackintoshes in German-language magazines was not exceptional, given their established interest in British work. Since the late 1880s the Germans and Austrians had been interested in British domestic architecture, for what they saw as its homely, individual and almost styleless quality, and in the simplicity, at once honest and artistic, of British Arts and Crafts. That interest continued until about 1908. Stylistically progressive architects like Ashbee, Voysey and Baillie Scott were particularly favoured, and the Mackintoshes had a place here too; but more traditional figures, such as Ernest Newton and Guy Dawber, were just as essential to the argument. The Mackintoshes' reputation in Germany and Austria has to be seen in this context. It started as part of this interest, but it was not exceptional. A short trawl through the internationally-minded German-language periodicals is enough to show that the Mackintoshes received less attention than Ashbee, Walter Crane, Baillie Scott and probably also Voysey, all of whom enjoyed much larger reputations than they did in other parts of Europe and in America. It will also show, incidentally, that progressive German and Austrian work was influenced much more by Baillie Scott, and possibly also by Ashbee and Voysey, than by the Mackintoshes.

134

120 Clock designed for The Hill House, 1905. Ebony and stained sycamore, with ivory inlay and painted numerals. This example was made for Mackintosh's own use.

Apart from the Berlin exhibition, Mackintosh had little work to do at the start of 1905 – only a shop-fitting job in Sauchiehall Street, and Scotland Street School where work had not got beyond the foundations. The sequence of commissions and opportunities which had stimulated so much creativity in the early 1900s seemed to falter. He carried on with humdrum and minor things. In March he laid out the plans of the Wellesley Tea Rooms in Sauchiehall Street, but someone else did the fittings. During the summer there were a pulpit, organcase, font and decorations to be seen to in Abbey Close Church in Paisley, and furniture for the drawing room at The Hill House, including a little clock. The clock shows how Mackintosh played games   120 with squares and light: in elevation, the hollow square of sixteen legs reads as five clear columns; at an angle, it is a dark forest.

Sketching in Norfolk on their summer holiday, Mackintosh ignored   121 mass and perspective, drawing linear elevations with small concentrations of detail, and sometimes other images piled on top, to a different scale. He seemed to be drawing his way lucidly through a technical problem and, at one and the same time, expressing some kind of conflict. In September, a client for a new house was in the offing, Francis Shand, assistant manager at the Nobels Explosives Company in Glasgow. Mackintosh sent him views of Windyhill and The Hill House. Shand seems to have replied that he wanted a house 'in one style', and Mackintosh wrote 'If you want a house in the Tudor or any other phase

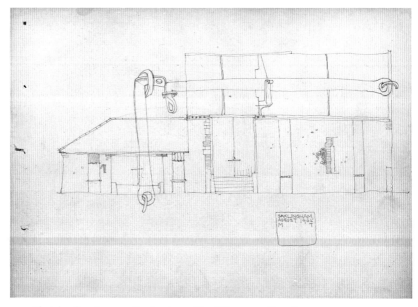

121 Sketch of outhouses, Saxlingham, Norfolk, 1905. Pencil.

of English architecture, I can promise you my best services.'[58] This does not sound like 'crawl – stumble – stagger – but go alone'.

By October the roof of Scotland Street School was on, and the Property Committee of the School Board were getting worried about Mackintosh's detailing. He wanted dark, perhaps black, glazed tiles for the walls and piers; at a meeting hurriedly arranged because he was leaving for Sussex, Mackintosh insisted on his scheme. A few days later the Committee decided to insist, in their turn, on the usual tiles; also on the usual window-glazing instead of Mackintosh's varied and smaller panes, and stair rails instead of Mackintosh's iron grating. On 31 October they visited the building and confirmed their findings.[59] In Sussex he sketched intensely, marking in the small panes which the School Board would not give him. In November he wrote claiming that the School Board had made a change of contract, leading the Chairman of the Board to thunder at Honeyman, Keppie and Mackintosh: 'I am directed to state that the board have no desire for controversy but the attitude taken by Mr Mackintosh in his interview with our committee and in his letter of the 4th instant left them no alternative but to state their position in clear terms . . .'[60] The work was done as the Board required.

Late in the year Miss Cranston proposed a tea room in the basement of her Argyle Street building, to be called the Dutch Kitchen. 122 That was the kind of work he wanted. He covered the surfaces with black–and–white chequers: linoleum on the floor, cut with the squares at right angles instead of the usual diagonal, infuriating the workmen, a finer pattern in the inglenook, finer still in the velvety dado, and strips and squares of the tiniest chequers defining the sharp right angles of the columns. There was nothing Dutch about it except the tiles in the fireplace; Vienna would have been nearer the mark. The Windsor chairs were enamelled bright green, and there was a touch of pink in the solitary window; everything else was black or white. There were curves in the inglenook but, as *The Studio* reported, 'Mackintosh adopts the square'.[61] This was not the square which we have seen at The Hill House and Hous'hill, articulating surfaces and generating forms singly or in groups, but the multiple square whose

122 Miss Cranston's Tea Rooms, 114 Argyle Street, Glasgow. The Dutch Kitchen, 1906.

tiny repeats created an air of glittering, hard-wearing chic. Until now the Mackintoshes' most memorable tea rooms had been light and feminine; the Dutch Kitchen, dark and stylish, was worthy to rank with them.

We can see now that the Mackintoshes' interiors followed a pattern, whereby a style was developed in a full domestic setting and then applied to exhibitions and tea rooms. We can see this happening in three stages: in 1900 the spare white interior with spots of colour was developed at Mains Street, and applied to the Vienna exhibit and the ladies' lunch room at Ingram Street. Between 1901 and 1903 a more ornate, colourful and curvilinear version was developed in the House for an Art Lover, and applied to the Turin exhibit and the Willow Tea Rooms. And in 1904–5 black and squares were developed in the lushness of The Hill House and the spareness of Hous'hill, and were then used in the Berlin exhibit and the Dutch Kitchen. This pattern is too neat — it overlooks austerity in parts of the Willow and whiteness at Hous'hill – but in these abundant years, clarity is welcome.

The abundance belongs to the relatively new world of furniture and interiors, in which Mackintosh and Margaret worked together. They dramatized the convention of dark/masculine and light/feminine, but the feminine predominated; the drawing rooms and bedrooms were the set pieces. Symbolic imagery, which had been a matter of watercolours and mysterious wording for Mackintosh in the 1890s, gave their furniture and decorations a new dimension. We have seen the vitality with which organic ornament endowed the furniture at Mains Street, and the sexual symbolism of the rose. And they brought everything under control, making the room itself a work of art. The result was a self-conscious revelation of the feminine or, to German and Austrian observers, a troubling mixture of spirituality and sensuality. But all the time, the formal language was changing. Mackintosh, more than Margaret, needed to develop new forms, and we have seen the phases of style through which their interiors moved, emerging in 1904–5 into a world of squares and clarity from which symbolism, spirituality, sensuality, and perhaps Margaret herself, had been excluded.

In Mackintosh's buildings, harling was the dominant theme. This austere material, which he first adopted at Windyhill as part of the language of Scottish domestic vernacular, lent itself to his most traditional and most modern effects. It is true that it banished his graceful mouldings of the 1890s onto the arms of chairs and the fronts of cupboards. But in return it offered him the soft geometry of overlapping and interpenetrating forms, which satisfied his taste for games and complexity. He used it in an all-over way, wrapping it over the gables instead of using coping stones, but it was never a unifying factor in his designs because at Windyhill and at The Hill House he was too much intent on variety. Harling may have been a purifying experience, however, for straight after The Hill House Mackintosh designed Scotland Street School, a stone building of great clarity whose mould-ings articulate the design as on no earlier building of his.

In all this it is hard to keep in touch with Mackintosh himself. These were busy and successful years, the peak of his career. He found kindred spirits in Vienna, and earned a reputation among the German and Austrian avant-garde. And in his native Glasgow he was far from overlooked. At The Hill House he had a wealthy and sympathetic client, and produced his domestic masterpiece, with which Blackie was well satisfied. At the Willow Tea Rooms, under similar patron-age, he produced interiors of such startling luxury and exclusiveness that Glasgow became a little Mackintosh-mad. And yet we do not know that he was happy. In 1903, with The Hill House and the Willow Tea Rooms both under construction, he told Anna Muthesius how 'antagonism and undeserved ridicule bring on feel-ings of despondency and despair'.[62] He thought of himself as a lonely artist struggling against the world. Perhaps, while he was designing to the top of his bent, the struggle could be sustained. But when the lull came in 1905, he was less sure. That he should be obstinate with the School Board was to be expected. But why did he write that worldly and complaisant letter to Francis Shand, saying that he would design his house in any phase of English architecture that he liked?

On 30 March 1906 Mackintosh bought 6 Florentine Terrace, Ann Street, for £925. (The house was later renumbered as 78 Ann Street and, later still, Ann Street was renamed Southpark Avenue.) It was a three-storey end-of-terrace house with an attic, dating from the 1850s, and typical of middle-class suburbs immediately surrounding the city centre. It was a stone's throw from the University and the street had its share of architects and university lecturers. We do not know exactly what made the Mackintoshes decide to leave their rented flat in the centre of the city and buy a house of their own. It probably fitted Margaret's middle-class expectations. And as for Mackintosh, it was part of the process of social betterment which had shaped his father's life and continued in his own. It was a step up in the world.

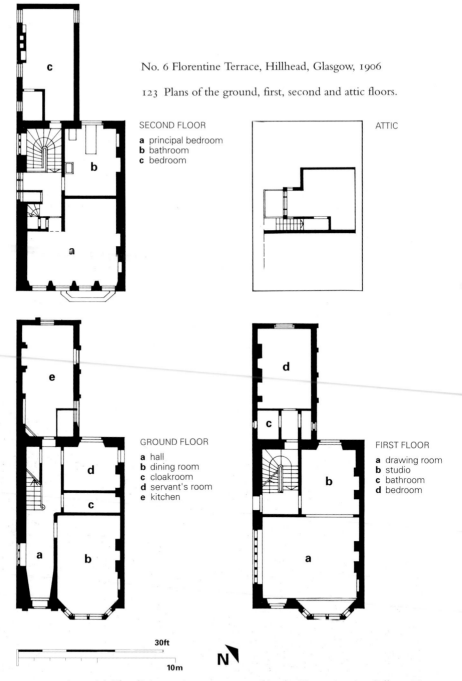

No. 6 Florentine Terrace, Hillhead, Glasgow, 1906

123 Plans of the ground, first, second and attic floors.

SECOND FLOOR

a principal bedroom
b bathroom
c bedroom

ATTIC

GROUND FLOOR

a hall
b dining room
c cloakroom
d servant's room
e kitchen

FIRST FLOOR

a drawing room
b studio
c bathroom
d bedroom

30ft

10m

124 (*opposite*) The dining room, reconstructed in the Hunterian Art Gallery, Glasgow.

CHAPTER FOUR

Crisis
Florentine Terrace 1906–1914

Between April and August 1906, there were workmen in 6 Florentine Terrace, making it ready for the *Künstlerpaar*. The dining room on the ground floor was decorated much as it had been at Mains Street, with the same fireplace and a dark paper below the frieze rail. But the frieze rail did not jump across the front of the windows, as it had at Mains Street and Hous'hill, and the walls were not articulated by slim posts, but by stencilled trellis patterns with roses weeping green and silver tears. Visitors to the reconstructed interiors in the Hunterian Art Gallery begin with the dining room and then go up the stairs; as they come into the studio-drawing room they gasp. They have moved from dark to light, experiencing the Mackintoshes' orchestration of the masculine/feminine convention.

They respond to the light which floods into the drawing room from the long south window which Mackintosh installed. It is reflected

125 No. 6 Florentine Terrace.
The drawing room,
reconstructed in the Hunterian
Art Gallery, Glasgow.

back by the white walls and white-enamelled woodwork. Here the
1850s mouldings were stripped away. The drawing-room fireplace
from Mains Street was put in. And the frieze rail ran round, brooking
no interruption, horizontalizing the room. When it came to the old,
upright windows at the front, it did not just leap across, it carried the
wall across too, blocking out the upper part of the windows, creating
a space in the bay which is both odd and familiar to us now, half
outside the room, half in. But the studio was handled differently: there
the bold cornice was retained and the frieze rail stopped to let the

window architrave pass, as it had at Mains Street. Elsewhere they kept the original staircase, ran the dining-room frieze rail from the head of the (probably) original doors, and left the dining-room windows untouched. Whether for reasons of cost, light or taste, the Mackintoshes did not gut 6 Florentine Terrace. It was a juxtaposition of new and old, like Mains Street.

In fact, it was very like Mains Street – the same tonalities, the same fireplaces, the same focus on the drawing room. Only the stencilling in the dining room, the more ruthless frieze rail, and the furniture

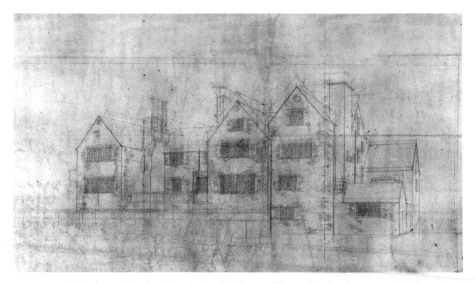

126 Perspective drawing for Auchinibert, Killearn, Stirlingshire, 1906–8. Pencil.

77, 80,
82 from schemes like Kingsborough Gardens and Turin were new. Stylistically, the place belonged to 1902–3. It was as if Hous'hill and the discipline of the square had never happened. Why did they reproduce Mains Street? One imagines that it was the work of Mackintosh and Margaret together. Was it because they could no longer be creative in collaboration?

126 Meanwhile the house for Francis Shand, which Mackintosh had said he would design in any phase of English architecture, was being built. It was called Auchinibert, and stood a little way above the village of Killearn, about 15 miles (24 kilometres) from Glasgow. The style was indeed English, derived from the stone-built vernacular of the Cotswolds or the Pennines. There were Mackintosh features inside and out, like the fluid moulding over the entrance. But it was essentially a decent, comfortable, inventively detailed, small country house, and could be mistaken for the work of any of Mackintosh's talented contemporaries. In the determinedly original world of Mackintosh's architecture, this suggests a loss of direction. It was as if the deliberate freedom of the Hill House façades had been given up. Stories of this date suggest a loosening grip: Thomas Howarth was told that on site visits Mackintosh spent too long in the pub at Killearn and not

144

enough on the job; he had a favourite seat there from which he could be dislodged 'only with the greatest difficulty'.[1]

On 27 September 1906 the Governors of Glasgow School of Art decided to complete their building, and appointed a Building Committee including three of Glasgow's most distinguished architects, J. J. Burnet, W. F. Salmon and David Barclay. There was no question of completing Mackintosh's original design; the School needed more accommodation and fire safety required more than one staircase. So the task was to complete the Renfrew Street range, to add a third tier of studios in Renfrew Street, and to design a new west wing and new staircases at either end of the building. On 1 February 1907 Honeyman, Keppie and Mackintosh were appointed architects 'on the understanding, that they are not at liberty to instruct any extra work or any alterations on the plans or specifications . . . without the written authority of the Building Committee'.[2] (A matter of over-spending at Scotland Street School was still being resolved.) Sketch plans were required by mid-March, but Mackintosh could not provide them in time, and they were not approved until 22 April. The completed plans were due on 10 June but Mackintosh wrote pleading 'pressure of other work'.[3] Deadlines were becoming a problem. Most of the plans were completed in June, and they were eventually passed by the local authority on 14 November. The barricades went up around the site the very next day.

The 'pressure of other work' may have come from another tea-room scheme. In 1907 Miss Cranston took over 217 Ingram Street. She now occupied the entire basement and ground floor of the Ingram Street building. In the summer Mackintosh designed the dark, 127

127 Miss Cranston's Tea Rooms, 205–217 Ingram Street, Glasgow. The Oak Room, 1907. The photograph shows the interior in September 1970, shortly before it was dismantled.

128 Square table for The Hill House, 1908. Ebonized pine with mother-of-pearl inlay.

127 galleried Oak Room, and it was completed around the end of the year. The gallery was carried on square timber columns which broke round the front into five uprights 'supporting' the ceiling; the uprights appeared through the gallery front, where laths were bent over them to form an undulating pattern. Wavy lines often accompanied Mackintosh's taste for the square, as a kind of embroidery, and here made up one of his directional games: they are wavy lines in perspective, but a perfect rectilinear lattice in elevation. The Miller Street frontage consisted of paired columns, like the ladies' lunch room facing into Ingram Street. There Mackintosh ran a frieze rail across the front of the windows. Here, he hung a whole gallery front across them. This is a kind of contradiction, for the pseudo-gallery blocks out the light.

While it was being built, the School of Art was threaded in and out of Mackintosh's life. On 5 February 1908 the Building Committee protested at unauthorized and extravagant works on the sub-basement porch and entrance. Five days later, Mackintosh's father died. On 26 February Mackintosh said he could make savings later, but the Committee insisted that he should keep the contract clearly before

128 him. In May he designed a low table for the drawing room at The Hill House which is the simplest and most complicated piece of furniture that he ever designed, a tribute to the generative power of the square. In October he dressed up as Morgan Le Fay for a fund-raising pageant at the University. By December the roof was on the School. In

146

129 Glasgow School of Art, 167 Renfrew Street, Glasgow. The completed building from the north-west.

January 1909 the Librarian and Building Committee objected that the library gallery in front of the windows would reduce light and serve little purpose. On 8 February, with none of the architect-members present, Mackintosh said new plans would be very expensive, and saved his design. In March, plastering and finishing began, and on 26 September Mackintosh reported that the extensions were practically completed. The School was formally reopened on 15 December 1909, when Sir John Stirling-Maxwell said Mackintosh would deserve well of his generation 'were it only because he had made them think'.[4]

The general view shows the finished building: the north front com- 129 pleted to the original design; the extra floor of studios set back behind the deep cornice and scarcely visible from the street; blankness on the west return as on the east, apart from three slightly cosmetic oriels; and the new west wing. In 1896–97 Mackintosh had proposed a

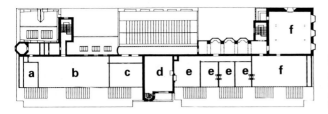

SECOND FLOOR

a studio, **b** embroidery room,
c composition room, **d** Headmaster's
studio, **e** professor's studio,
f composition room

100ft

N

30m

MEZZANINES

a life room, **b** library balcony, **c** room over
library balcony

FIRST FLOOR

a design room, **b** antique room,
c Headmaster's room, **d** life room,
e museum, **f** library

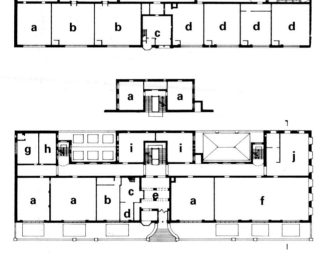

MEZZANINE

a lunch room

GROUND FLOOR

a ornament room, **b** board room,
c materials store, **d** office, **e** entrance
hall, **f** junior architecture, **g** male
teachers' room, **h** female teachers'
room, **i** cloakroom, **j** senior
architecture

MEZZANINE

a caretaker's house (upper floor),
b cloakroom

BASEMENT

a living-animal modelling, **b** ceramics,
c silversmithing, **d** metalwork and
enamelling, **e** stained glass, wood
carving and weaving, **f** heating chamber,
g coals, **h** boiler house, **i** antique modelling room, **j** ornament modelling room,
k life modelling room (evening),
l caretaker's house (lower floor),
m anatomy room, **n** store, **o** life modelling
room (day), **p** lecture theatre

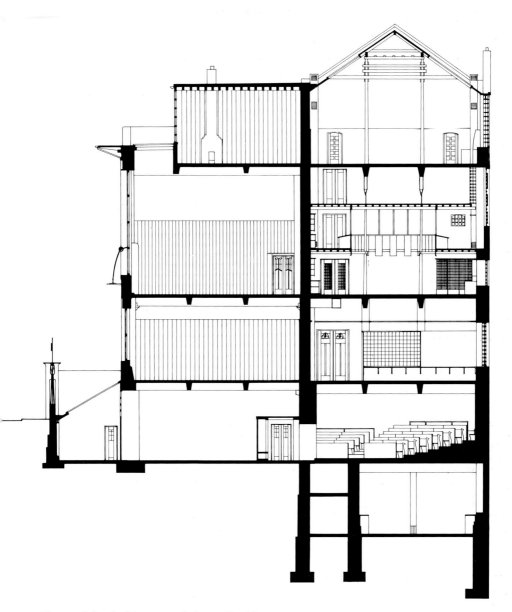

Glasgow School of Art, second phase of building, 1907–9

130 Plans of the basement, ground, first and second floors, with mezzanines.

131 Section through the westernmost studios and west wing, as marked on the ground-floor plan in Ill. 130.

132 Glasgow School of Art. The west wing.

picturesque treatment here, roughly matching the east wing. But since then, at Scotland Street and Hous'hill, he had passed through a cold fire and he was ruthless. The west front of this wing consists of three identical oriel windows, each about 63 feet (19 metres) high, under a gable; the oriel is a traditional form, but 63 feet is not a traditional height. As the section shows, this façade, whose verticality would do justice to a cathedral, fronts a horizontal arrangement of five floors and two mezzanines. It is about as different as could be from the north front. But then discontinuity was already the language of the School of Art.

132

131

The quality of the oriels depends upon the smooth transitions from stonework to windows and back again, and on the close texture of the iron glazing bars which makes the windows ambivalent. In the photograph opposite the windows look almost solid; in the general view they are light and insubstantial. Thus Mackintosh sustained two interdependent but contradictory meanings. From one angle the oriel is a single form which runs up the building regardless of stone or glass; from another it is two startlingly different materials. These meanings are clearest at the top, where the tiny windows slice through the stonework.

132

129

What is there and what is not there is a constant theme. The largest windows are framed by architraves and flanked by stone cylinders, oval in plan, that were intended for sculpted figures, but the sculpture was

133 Glasgow School of Art. Entrance in Scott Street.

Glasgow School of Art

134 The library in about 1909, looking towards the door.

135 Light fittings in the library.

cut from the budget. Just below each window the architrave forms the head of a semi-circular niche, which is empty: this is a Mannerist conceit. The back of the School was covered with harling, and the brief forbade projections beyond the building line. So Mackintosh took the projections of the west front and buried them in the wall. On this façade, the ground-floor oriels are almost submerged in harling, the upper parts more exposed, as if Mackintosh was inviting us to complete an excavation.

The basement entrance is a tour-de-force of forms in which Mackintosh seems to lay hold of Mannerism with one hand and Expressionism with the other, while still playing his own particular games. At the top there is a negative multiple architrave stepped back into the wall, and then the architrave proper stepped like a ziggurat. The cylinders embraced by the architrave and the course of stone above the lintel are worked as if for sculpture, but the course has a curved recess in the middle – a negative cylinder. And under that is a hole which is both a niche without sculpture and a negative keystone. 133

The entrance leads to a flight of stairs full of inventive Mackintosh details, and the stairs lead to the library, which is the core of the new building. It looks complicated, partly because the gallery structure wants more space than the room can offer; but the basic structure is simple. A central space is flanked by two rows of four wooden uprights, standing over two rolled steel joists. The lower part of the uprights consists of three members; paired wooden beams run between the walls and the outer members to support the gallery, which is set back 3 feet (90 centimetres). The central member rises 134–136 into the darkness to meet – but not to support – the suspended ceiling. It is as simple as that. Decorative features like the short balustrades between gallery and uprights, which are chamfered and enamelled in primary colours, create the complexity. Mackintosh was obliged to support the gallery on the line of the structural metalwork, and may have been wise to set it back. But all the rest is a grove of trees, a place between darkness and light, the playful subdivision of space, construction that is not construction at all. This is the not the last, but it is certainly the greatest of Mackintosh's timber fantasies, and his fullest tribute to Japan.

135 The light fittings in the centre of the library are another kind of fantasy. Like many of Mackintosh's light fittings, they were made of metal crudely pierced, shaped and soldered together. The placing of his fittings had always been careful, but the design was not particularly adventurous until the cascade of coloured glass that is the chandelier in the Salon de Luxe. The library lights are that chandelier transformed by the generative power of the square. The inner, stepped forms and outer, rectangular bands create spatial relationships of there-and-not-there on a tiny scale.

Looking towards the oriel windows, we see three vertical bands of hazy light, and a dark band running across them. This is the fourth

136 Glasgow School of Art. The library in about 1909, looking towards the oriel windows.

137 Glasgow School of Art. Looking up into one of the oriel windows, from the floor of the library, past the gallery, to internal glazing on the floor above.

side of the gallery. The Librarian and Building Committee had objected, but Mackintosh was engaged in his most peculiar game. He designed three great, light-giving oriels and then crossed them out. This was the culmination of all those frieze rails running across windows, and a stronger version of the pseudo-gallery in the Oak Room. It was as if Mackintosh was externalizing some strange and radical contradiction in himself.

The floor by the oriels is, and always has been, occupied by the heating system, so you cannot walk into them. But you can poke your head into the wells of light, into the gap between the vertical outside 137 and the horizontal inside of the building. This is a related game, the culmination of so much: the strange misfit between side gallery and pseudo-transept at Queen's Cross, the paired columns at Ingram Street, the room within a music room in the Art-Lover's House, the staircase wells at Scotland Street School, and the drawing-room bay at 102

Florentine Terrace. Mackintosh had discovered that plan and elevation do not have to go hand in hand, that there could be a gap between them, in which he loved to play. It was a strange notion, quite different from the real separation between external wall and internal structure which steel-frame construction made possible at this time. In the mid-Victorian buildings of Alexander Thomson the windows are often set back and separate from the structural uprights, like two layers, and Mackintosh's notion may have started there.

Robert Macleod, an expert on Mackintosh, wrote that 'There is no element in the building which cannot be related, directly or indirectly, to contemporary British work.'[5] By this he meant English work: Charles Holden's Central Library in Bristol of 1902–6, Holden's premises for the British Medical Association (now Zimbabwe House) in the Strand, London, of 1906–8, and Belcher and Joass's Royal Insurance building on the corner of St James's Street and Piccadilly, London, of 1907–8. Mackintosh's design is Mannerist in spirit as the two London buildings are, and the conceit of the empty niche was shared with, though probably not borrowed from, the building in Piccadilly. But more obvious exemplars for Mackintosh's design lie closer at hand: it is also a very Glaswegian building. The seven- and eight-storey office blocks of contemporary Glasgow often had bays and oriel windows of this height, which were derived in their turn from the commercial buildings of Chicago in the 1890s; the curved base of Mackintosh's oriels, in fact, recalls the Monadnock Building in Chicago of 1889–91, by Burnham and Root. At the same time, the plainness of Mackintosh's oriels and their smooth transition from masonry to glazing can be found in the canted bays which were used at the back of contemporary Glasgow offices to maximize light from the narrow lanes. The peculiarity of Mackintosh's School of Art design is to have three such oriels ranked close together on a principal street front, with uninterrupted glazing reaching a vertical height of 24 feet (7.3 metres) though he had reached about 18 feet (5.5 metres) on the bays at Scotland Street.

This design stands out in Mackintosh's work like a rock, or perhaps like one of his beloved tower-houses. At a time when he seemed to be losing direction – witness the backward-looking Florentine Terrace and the alien competence of Auchinibert – Mackintosh produced his boldest design. Perhaps he had been working on it ever since 1897, going over the familiar, sloping site in his mind with each new job. Perhaps the commission to complete the building put him back in touch with some old daring.

138 John A. Campbell: 157–167 Hope Street, Glasgow, 1902–3.

Which is painful to relate, for the completion of the School of Art was followed by four-and-a-half empty years. Between 1910 and the outbreak of the First World War, only six new jobs can be firmly attributed to Mackintosh, none of them large or of the first rank. It is not clear why this was. According to Thomas Howarth, Mackintosh drank a lot at this time and began to lose interest in the practice. 'We are told by those who worked with him that his lunch hour often lasted from 1 o'clock to 4.45 p.m. . . . . At times his directions became vague and purposeless.'[6] But this is to overlook the circumstances. The financial records of Honeyman, Keppie and Mackintosh suggest that work coming into the office was halved in 1910 and halved again in 1911, only picking up in 1914; Keppie seems to have suffered in this as much as Mackintosh. It may be that the loss of work was something Mackintosh could do little about; and perhaps it was that which led to heavy drinking, rather than the other way about. And can we assume, anyway, that Mackintosh's drinking belonged only to these fallow years? Nikolaus Pevsner, who talked to people in the 1930s about Mackintosh, thought it came earlier, and was an inspiration:

'During his best years, I have been told, he sometimes arrived at the office in the evening with piles of sheets of paper, ready to fill them during the night either with sketches or with large-scale details drawn with the greatest possible accuracy. In the morning they would find him exhausted and drunk, and the sheets of paper covered with drawings so perfect that they might have been jewels.'[7] Perhaps drink reinforced Mackintosh's moods, inspiring him when he was busy, deepening his gloom when he was not.

There was plenty to be gloomy about. The policeman's son had invested so much in art, in reputation, in working with Margaret. And he had been rewarded with success, at first. But now, when work dried up, there was a kind of void. It is a pity that he and Margaret never had children, for they would have filled the void better than drink. But the Mackintoshes were, and remained, childless.

There were no new designs in 1910, just the completion of interiors at Hous'hill and Ingram Street, and additions to a cottage near Kilmacolm. In 1911 Mackintosh designed the interior of the White Cockade Tea Room for Miss Cranston at Glasgow's Scottish National Exhibition, but no sign ficant evidence survives of it. And in the summer he redecorated the men's tea room at Ingram Street as the Chinese Room. The ceiling was painted dark, the walls were lined with canvas, and screens of latticework were used to panel the walls, divide the room, and create a false ceiling. Within the latticework there were curved niches of mirror-glass or a plastic material; fretwork and pagoda-like details supplied the Chinese motif; and the whole thing was painted a strong blue. Using the simplest means, Mackintosh created a dark, exotic atmosphere similar to the Moorish and Oriental interiors then common in male places of refreshment or entertainment, such as smoking rooms. Fantasy, glitter and overstatement, which have a place in tea rooms, came more easily to him in this thematic, male interior than it had in the white, stylized domesticity of the ladies' lunch room a few yards away. The Cloister Room at Ingram Street, decorated by Mackintosh about six months later with strips of lozenges like a pierrot and mirror-glass in niches, was almost equally exotic, though some of the motifs derived from modern Vienna.[8]

In 1912 and 1913 Mackintosh's executed architectural work consisted only of a ladies' hairdressing salon in Union Street, Glasgow, and alterations and additions to a couple of houses near Kilmacolm. One large and important project, however, occupied his attention, the competition entry for a teacher training college, hostel and

139 Miss Cranston's Tea Rooms, 205–217 Ingram Street, Glasgow. The Chinese Room, 1911. The photograph was taken in 1950.

demonstration school in the Glasgow suburb of Jordanhill. But as the deadline approached, he had only a few inadequate tracings to show. The job was taken out of his hands, and in about June 1913 he resigned from the partnership. He set up an office of his own, but no work came his way.

He was now a very lonely architect. While he had been exploring the relationship of curves and squares in the chambers of his imagination, British architecture had moved away from the cult of the individual, the decorative and the domestic that had been so strong in the 1890s. Progressive architects adopted a stricter, more impersonal discipline, for which Classicism was the appropriate language. Mackintosh was out of date. He must have been galled to read a review of his new School of Art building in a student magazine which described it as 'bizarre'.[9] Mackintosh had used Classical forms lightly and effectively at Scotland Street School. But in 1906 he designed crazily individual Ionic pilasters for the new board room of the School of Art, as if cocking a snook at the new orthodoxy. Orthodoxy or not, Classicism was the form of modernity in 1910, and if one architect in Britain epitomized this fact, it was a member of the School of Art Building Committee, J. J. Burnet. Burnet's work exemplified the range and modernity of Edwardian Classicism, for it included, on the one hand, the steel-frame and early concrete-slab construction of McGeoch's ironmongery warehouse, where a minutely controlled Edwardian Baroque was combined with a verticality inspired by Louis Sullivan, and on the other, the refined and monumental Edward VII Galleries added to the British Museum in 1906–14. It cannot have been easy for Mackintosh, at this stage in his career, to think about Burnet.

Classicism was also the way forward for progressive architects in Germany and Austria, including Mackintosh's admirers. Olbrich died in 1908, but his later works were Classical in spirit. Classicism led Behrens towards the rational-monumental factory buildings he designed in Berlin from 1908, which are crucial in the history of Modernism. And as for Hoffmann, his interest in Biedermeier and in Mediterranean vernacular buildings had always made him a potential Classicist. His houses entered a Classical phase in 1905–6. Mary Sturrock was shown round some of them in Vienna in 1914 and was

140 J. J. Burnet: McGeoch's Ironmongery Warehouse, 28 West Campbell Street, Glasgow, 1905.

140

141 Francis Newbery: *The Building Committee of the Glasgow School of Art*, 1913–14. Oil on canvas.

disappointed to find him 'entirely Biedermeierish. He said "Of course I was influenced by Mackintosh when I was younger, but that was many years ago." '[10]

All this hurt. At this period, Walter Blackie called on Mackintosh in his solitary office. 'I found Mackintosh sitting at his desk, evidently in a deeply depressed frame of mind. To my enquiry as to how he was keeping and what he was doing he made no response. But presently he began to talk slowly and dolefully. He said how hard he found it to receive no general recognition; only a very few saw merit in his work and the many passed him by.'[11]

At about this time too, Francis Newbery painted a group portrait of the Building Committee of Glasgow School of Art, sitting round the table in their Mackintosh-designed board room. In February 1914 he offered to present it to the School. The presentation was fixed for May, but when it was unveiled, it was clear that Newbery had added

141

to it. On the left, just in the group but certainly not of it, was the figure of Charles Rennie Mackintosh. Nothing expresses his professional isolation so well as this painting, and the way in which it was painted.

In the middle of July the Mackintoshes went on holiday to Walberswick, a Suffolk fishing village popular with artists. Francis Newbery had a semi-detached villa there, and the Mackintoshes stayed in the other half. About three weeks later, war broke out. They might have gone back but, as Margaret later told Anna Geddes, 'I induced Toshie to just stop on & get the real rest cure that he has so badly needed for quite two years.'[12] Then she went up to Glasgow, let 6 Florentine Terrace for a year, and came back to Walberswick. In the Mackintosh myth, the hero, ground down by lack of work and recognition, decides to leave Glasgow for good; he shuts up his house and turns his back on his native city.[13] The truth is not very different from this; but the difference is important. Mackintosh had plenty of work and plenty of recognition in Glasgow in the early 1900s. And then, in the years covered by this chapter, things went wrong. New directions in architecture left him isolated and apparently old-fashioned. Honeyman, Keppie and Mackintosh were short of work. And Mackintosh fell into some kind of depression. But at no point did the Mackintoshes decide to leave Glasgow. They were away when the war broke out and, somehow, they never went back.

CHAPTER FIVE

Loss and Gain
Walberswick and Chelsea 1914–1923

In Walberswick Jessie Newbery had fixed them up with a studio, just a fisherman's shed looking out over the estuary. Margaret was working, with her husband's help, on two big panels in oil, on the theme of the 65th Psalm: 'Thou crownest the year with thy goodness . . . and the little hills rejoice on every side . . . the valleys also are covered over with corn; they shout for joy, they also sing.' Here, on the flat and crumbling Suffolk coast, with winter coming on, she painted a hymn in praise of nature and fruitfulness. The babies are unpleasantly pig-like, but the painting is clear. The soft, introverted atmosphere of her earlier paintings is gone, and there is a kind of deliberate joy. She was fifty.

    And Mackintosh was working alongside her. He was making flower drawings, thinking perhaps of publishing them as a set. This was something which went back to the earliest times and his father's gardening, before the struggles for recognition, before 'design'. He would sometimes draw flowers on sketching trips and holidays, and his sketchbooks of the 1890s contain pencil drawings of extraordinary

142

142 Margaret Macdonald Mackintosh, with Charles Rennie Mackintosh: *The Little Hills*, 1914. Oil on canvas.

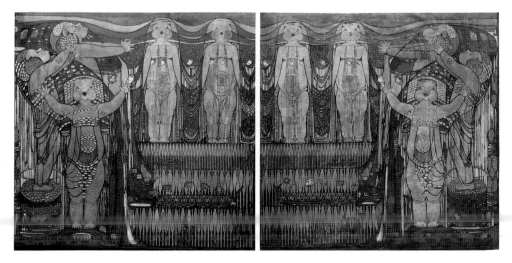

accuracy, done in outline with occasional hatching. In the 1900s, with the richness of his talent on him, he became more ambitious, putting in washes of watercolour here and there, and arranging the flowers, sometimes, for decorative effect more than accuracy.

He produced over forty drawings at Walberswick and they were his whole work there; but he did not take the decorative element any further. He drew the fritillary because he liked its chequerwork, but he drew it accurately. These drawings stand in the long tradition of European botanical illustration, in which flowers are set, specimen-like, in the centre of a plain background. Mackintosh told William Davidson they were 'quite straightforward frank work'.[1] His appetite for new forms, which in Glasgow had fed so hungrily on tables and chairs, was somehow given pause. He was content to look at nature, and to play. In January Margaret wrote to Anna Geddes: 'Already Toshie is quite a different being and evidently at the end of the year will be quite fit again.'[2]

He worked from freshly-cut specimens, mostly of cultivated flowers, and we can picture him leaning over the walls of Walberswick gardens, begging a sprig of aubretia or winter stock. He must have seemed odd. Old men in Walberswick remember how he went for walks in the dark, looking like Sherlock Holmes in a black tweed cape and deerstalker. One boy thought he was a detective and followed him, but Mackintosh just went down to the beach and stood for a long time, looking out to sea. 'He didn't seem to notice the waves washing round his boots.'[3] Mary Sturrock, who knew the Mackintoshes better, remembered their dignity: 'whatever they really felt, they didn't show it.'[4]

The people of Walberswick were used to artists, and would have accepted eccentricities in normal times. But someone learnt that Mackintosh had worked in Germany and Austria. With his strange accent and nightly walks, he must be a spy. In early May the military authorities came, took away papers, including letters from Germany and Austria, kept them for five weeks, and then served an order on Mackintosh to leave the area. Margaret fell ill with worry and Mackintosh, who was fiercely patriotic, went up to London to clear his name.

In London he found some temporary work with Patrick Geddes, and there was a possibility of work in India, but nothing came of it. In early August 1915 Margaret joined him, and they found two studios next door to each other in Glebe Place, Chelsea. These were to be the focus of their lives for the next eight years. They took

143 *Fritillaria, Walberswick*, 1915. Pencil and watercolour.

lodgings nearby, and in the evenings they would usually eat at the Blue Cockatoo, an incompetent restaurant on Cheyne Walk favoured by artists. Here they met many of those who were to become their friends.

There was the painter J. D. Fergusson whom they had known in Glasgow, now back in England after years in Paris and the south of France where he had become, virtually, a Fauve – well before Roger Fry's Post-Impressionist exhibitions of 1910 and 1912. There was his partner, the dancer Margaret Morris, who ran an avant-garde theatre club in Flood Street where Mackintosh and Margaret were welcomed. And there were other painters, James Pryde, Randolph Schwabe and George Sheringham, the musicians Clifford Bax and Eugene Goossens, and the photographer Emil Otto Hoppé, who worked in both fashionable and avant-garde circles. These were some of their closest friends, all Chelsea people, all creative, and all younger than the Mackintoshes.

Something important had changed in the Mackintoshes' lives. In Glasgow their radicalism had been expressed in their work while their lives had been deliberately, aesthetically bourgeois. It was the essence of those kempt white interiors at 120 Mains Street to combine radical and bourgeois values. But since then, perhaps in Mackintosh's drinking, perhaps on the Suffolk coast, they had lost their bourgeois identity. Now, in their bleak studios, with little money, little prospect of work, and new young friends, they were becoming Bohemians.

And the friendships help us to understand their work. The painters were often decorators and designers, crossing and re-crossing the boundaries as Mackintosh liked. Fergusson probably helped Mackintosh to a looser, more adventurous technique in his paintings, and stronger, brighter colours. They liked mingling the arts, and most of them were involved in 'The Plough', a theatre group which met at Hoppé's house, 'mostly artists musicians and other mad hatters' as Margaret wrote.[5] The Mackintoshes designed sets for two of their productions. And they seemed to hover on the edge of developments in art. Chelsea and the New English Art Club had been replaced as the focus of the avant-garde by Bloomsbury, Camden Town and the Vorticists, and the essential avant-garde exhibiting body was the London Group. Some of their friends showed with the London Group. But Mackintosh exhibited with the International Society of Sculptors, Painters and Engravers and the Friday Club, and he helped to reorganize the London 'Salon of the Independants' after the war. Like Chelsea itself, these groups had seen more radical days.

Some months after they moved into Glebe Place, Mackintosh was asked by Wenman J. Bassett-Lowke to alter a terrace house in Northampton. Bassett-Lowke was an interesting man. He was a manufacturer of engineering models and model railway engines – elderly model railway enthusiasts are still moved by the name of Bassett-Lowke. The company was doing war work and making large profits; Bassett-Lowke was looking around himself. He was a member of the Fabian Society, and joined the Design and Industries Association in 1916. He was a particular admirer of George Bernard Shaw. He had a sense of machinery and how things fit together. He liked living in the country as well as the town. And he liked modernity. In fact he was the perfect English Modernist. Rising forty and soon to be married, he was looking for an architect with modern ideas. On holiday in Cornwall in 1915, he met a friend from Glasgow who enthused about Mackintosh, so he sought him out.

Bassett-Lowke had bought 78 Derngate, an early 19th-century terrace house in the oldest part of Northampton. It was small, with two rooms on each of three floors and a kitchen in the basement, and the front parlour was tiny. Mackintosh's job was to put in a bathroom, make some more space, especially in the parlour, and furnish and decorate. Put like that, it sounds like a small job, and yet it was one of the most remarkable of his career. Inside, he took the staircase and moved it through ninety degrees so that it ran across the middle of the house. The parlour was now shallower but much wider, and it was known as the hall, or lounge hall. Outside, he added a rustic-looking bay window to the street front, for he did not share the enthusiasm of some English architects for the practicality and dignity of the late Georgian urban vernacular.

The house was four storeys high at the back, and here Mackintosh added a three-storey bay which enlarged the kitchen in the basement and the dining room, and gave a deep covered balcony to the principal bedroom and a balcony to the guest bedroom above. Derngate is in the centre of Northampton, but the back of the house faced south over the River Nene, and the view was almost rural: the Bassett-Lowkes liked to breakfast on their balcony. White, rectilinear, unmoulded, and designed for fresh air and the sun, this small extension was as near as Mackintosh, or anyone in Britain at this date, came to the cool, white rationalism of the European Modern Movement.

Cool, white and rational, however, the inside of 78 Derngate was not. The hall was painted black, dull, velvety black, and all the furniture was black as well. Light from the new bay window fell on the

147

148

144

144 No. 78 Derngate, Northampton, 1916–17. The hall.

fireplace with its books and flowers and bust of Shaw. The few unen-
cumbered stretches of wall were divided into bays by strips of black
and white chequerwork, with blocks of stencilling superimposed on
them at frieze level, so that they look like rectilinear trees. The stencils consisted of dense, overlapping triangles in gold, grey, vermilion,
145   blue, green and white. A screen of black latticed squares ran across the
back of the room, against the stairs. The latticework was partly open
and partly solid, and some of the solid squares were filled with
chevrons, squares and triangles in coloured glass. The floor was stained
black, with a carpet of black-and-white chequerwork. The ceiling
was black as well, except for a white rose from which hung a corona
decorated with brightly-coloured chevrons, like some enormous
savage necklace. This room was used as a sitting room, though the
only things to sit on were a black Chinese-looking settle in the bay,
with petunia-coloured cushions, and four black Chinese-looking hall
chairs.

168

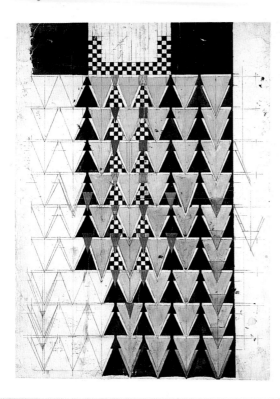

No. 78 Derngate

145 Design for stencil decorations in the hall, 1916. Pencil and watercolour.

146 Duplicates of the guest bedroom furniture, 1917, made for Sydney Horstmann of Fairlawn, Weston Road, Bath. (The original Derngate suite is at present untraced.) The fabric on the wash-stand is by Phoebe McLeish, replacing a Mackintosh-designed textile.

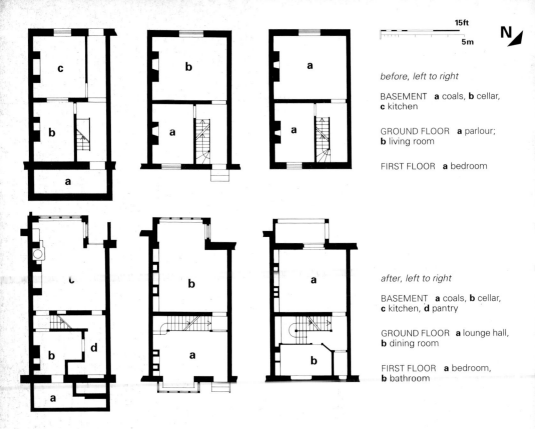

before, left to right

BASEMENT **a** coals, **b** cellar,
c kitchen

GROUND FLOOR **a** parlour;
b living room

FIRST FLOOR **a** bedroom

after, left to right

BASEMENT **a** coals, **b** cellar,
c kitchen, **d** pantry

GROUND FLOOR **a** lounge hall,
b dining room

FIRST FLOOR **a** bedroom,
b bathroom

147 No. 78 Derngate. Plans of three of the four floors, illustrating Mackintosh's alterations.

In the rest of the house a different atmosphere prevailed. In the dining room, Mackintosh designed the fireplace and fitted cupboards in walnut, while Bassett-Lowke designed the plain circular dining table and chairs. The main bedroom was papered in grey, with severe rectilinear furniture in sycamore, relying for effect on the quartered grain of the wood and a few strips of black inlay. In the guest bedroom upstairs the mahogany furniture was equally severe, but decorated with inlaid squares instead of strips. These rooms could not have been more different from the white, intimate bedrooms at Mains Street or The Hill House. The bathroom and kitchen had American fittings of the latest type, and the kitchen was lit by bulkhead lights as used in ships. All this was minutely planned by Bassett-Lowke in readiness for his wedding in March 1917. We do not know what part his bride, Florence Jones, played in the preparations for her future home.

146

148 No. 78 Derngate. The garden front, with Florence Bassett-Lowke.

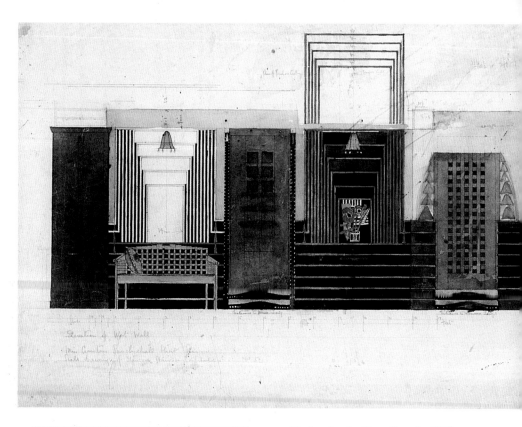

149 Design for the Dug-Out, the Willow Tea Rooms, 217 Sauchiehall Street, Glasgow, 1917. Pencil and watercolour.

150 Ladderback armchair from the Dug-Out, 1917. Ebonized wood.

151 *Anemones*, c. 1916. Pencil and watercolour. The frame in the background contains, not a mirror, but an alternative composition, incorporating a similar vase of flowers and a version of one of Mackintosh's textile designs.

152 A textile design, probably for a furnishing fabric, c. 1916. Pencil and watercolour.

No. 78 Derngate actually feels like the product of two minds, both male: in the hall there was dazzling darkness; in the rest of the house, quiet good sense, quality of materials and technological modernism, none of which had ever interested Mackintosh. Client and architect were not at odds, for Bassett-Lowke came back to Mackintosh for more, as we shall see. But Mackintosh had never worked with anyone who knew so much about design before. It all makes sense if we suppose that Bassett-Lowke was very much in charge, that Mackintosh designed all that severe post-Arts and Crafts bedroom furniture to suit Bassett-Lowke's taste, and that Bassett-Lowke gave him a free hand in the hall, so as to proclaim his own (Bassett-Lowke's) modernity. As for the white bay at the back, that also may be Bassett-Lowke's, for he seems to have disliked the usual British type of open balcony as being too small and giving no protection from the weather. Mackintosh's balconies both before and after Derngate were of precisely that sort.

The hall does not suggest that Mackintosh had lost his nerve in the five years since he had last designed an interior, though it is not so consciously inserted into the existing building as the interiors at 120 Mains Street, Hous'hill and 6 Florentine Terrace had been. It is startling, assured, almost obsessive. The Chinese Room and the Cloister Room at Ingram Street had been his last interiors in Glasgow, and Derngate has much in common with them: the dark walls, the bright colours of the frieze, the latticework, the stepped and Chinese profiles. But the triangles, which were almost the *leitmotif* of the hall, were new.

Mackintosh had used triangles in a small way at Ingram Street, the *Daily Record* building and Scotland Street School. Now they were everywhere, challenging the square as his favourite motif. They came, unquestionably, from Vienna, from Moser possibly or from the work of Josef Urban which had been illustrated in *The Studio's* special number, *The Art-Revival in Austria* (1906).[6] Mackintosh's squares were stable; they allowed him to play with the alternation of solid and void, the balance of plain and ornamented parts. Here, his triangles are dynamic; they are not equilateral, they have one sharpest point; at times they seem to stab. In the design for the stencils they look like barbed spears, dipped in blood. And when brought together in the frieze, they generate intricate, repetitive movements, like a fairground automaton. There had been movement in Mackintosh's ornament round 1900, but it had been organic; now it was mechanical.

The hall at Derngate reveals some interesting shifts in Mackintosh's

139

145

174

taste. In the old days he and Margaret had made the middle-class convention of dark/masculine – light/feminine into something very special. At Derngate he painted the room which was used as a sitting room, and so by convention feminine, black. And whereas, in the early 1900s, he and Margaret had experimented on domestic interiors and then transferred them to tea rooms, the Derngate hall transferred the exotic and quite undomestic style he had adopted in the Chinese and Cloister Rooms at Ingram Street to a house.

As if to underline this point, Mackintosh designed another interior towards the end of the Derngate work. The ceilings were painted shiny black. And the surviving designs show dark walls striped and banded with colour, square latticework, black or brightly coloured furniture, and a fireplace decorated with spiky zig-zags and lozenges in red, blue, yellow and green, like a multi-coloured Alpine range. It was the formula of the Derngate hall, but it was done for the Dug-Out, a basement addition to Miss Cranston's Willow Tea Rooms.

The furniture for the Dug-Out is typical of Mackintosh's later work, not least in the thread of eclecticism which runs through it. There is hardly an inch of the ladderback chair that does not proclaim its source in traditional furniture. It is narrow at the back and broad at the front like a traditional Scottish caqueteuse; there is the stepped ladderback itself; the arms have a faintly Chinese air; and they are attached to the frame with cube-and-bobbin detail. It also seems to have been designed for someone very short in the leg and very long in the upper arm.

Derngate and the Dug-Out were commissions like those of the Glasgow years; but they were almost all Mackintosh got during the four years of the war. He had time to paint flowers again, and began a series of ambitious compositions in watercolour, quite different from the botanical drawings at Walberswick. The flowers are luxuriant blooms which look as if they came from a florist in the King's Road, Chelsea, and they are presented in the traditional manner of still-lifes, in a vase on a table at the front of the picture. Their strong colour suggests the influence of Post-Impressionist and Fauve work, but they are very precisely drawn. There are only about a dozen of them, and they seem to be close to the heart of Mackintosh's development. In them he could explore a new visual world without the restraints of practical decorative art. After his professional world collapsed in Glasgow, Mackintosh's instinct as an architect and designer was probably to rebuild it, and he might have done so if war had not intervened. His instinct as a painter, on the other hand, was to accept the painful

149

150

151

153 No. 78 Derngate, Northampton. The guest bedroom of 1919, reconstructed in the Hunterian Art Gallery, Glasgow.

freedom, and explore. At Walberswick he had turned to flower drawings for healing, looking at nature. Now, in the city, responsive to the fashions of the avant-garde, he was exploring a new and sophisticated world of painterly composition and saturated, vibrant colour.

The influence of these watercolours can be felt in the designs for printed textiles which the Mackintoshes began to produce in these years, offering them to manufacturers at between six and ten guineas each. This was a new departure, in which they may have been advised by Claud Lovat Fraser, or by George Sheringham and E. O. Hoppé who were doing similar work. For neither Mackintosh nor Margaret had much experience of working for manufacturers, and their decorative textiles had always been stencilled or embroidered. Probably several hundred designs were produced, more by Mackintosh than by Margaret, and many were bought by William Foxton of London, an enthusiast for vivid colour, modern designs and the marriage of art and industry. Few actual fabrics are known to survive.

152

Some designs are floral, and seem to grow out of Mackintosh's new watercolours, others are geometrical like the Derngate frieze. The majority are somewhere in between, with abstract-organic motifs – swirls, meanders and asymmetrical blobs. They show the richness and freedom Mackintosh was learning from contemporary painting, but are also typical of the period, the strong colours reminiscent of Bakst and the Ballets Russes, the patterns comparable with the work of Foxton's other designers, such as Minnie McLeish, and with German and Viennese pattern designs Mackintosh would have seen in *The Studio Year-Book of Decorative Art*. Almost none of them could be mistaken for work of earlier than 1910, and perhaps the drawing reflects the contemporary enthusiasm for primitive art introduced rather forcibly into the decorative arts by Roger Fry's Omega Workshops from 1913. It would be important at this time for Mackintosh to recover primitive force.

As the war came to an end, Mackintosh and Margaret must have hoped for better times. But they were slow to come. On 1 April 1919 he wrote to William Davidson: 'I find myself at the moment very hard up and I was wondering if you could see your way to buy one of my flower pictures or lanscapes for £20 or £30. . . . I am just about to start some work that will bring me in a fair remuneration. . . . I shall be glad to hear from you this week as my rent of £16 is overdue and I must pay or leave.'[7] Davidson sent £30 and Mackintosh wrote on 5 April to thank him, 'I enclose some "Poster" stamps which I did for Bassett-Lowke. If you know any business man who would like such a

154 Design for an advertising label for Bassett-Lowke Ltd., *c.* 1918. Pencil and watercolour.

stamp I shall be glad to make a design.'[8] Bassett-Lowke had provided a trickle of small jobs in 1918–19; the textile designs brought in something; there was rent from 6 Florentine Terrace; and Margaret had a small private income. But it was not enough. In August Mackintosh wrote again to Davidson: 'I fully expected that I would be out of the wood by this time but alas I am still very hard pressed to make both ends meet. If you propose taking some of the pictures could you please wire me £7 this week as I have a tax to pay that must be settled at once or the law will move.'[9] Davidson, who cared about the Mackintoshes, wired the money.

The work which Mackintosh was about to start may have been new furniture and decorations for the guest bedroom at 78 Derngate, which seem to belong to the second half of 1919. Mackintosh designed a canopy of black-and-white striped paper edged, and in places overlaid, by ultramarine ribbon. The stripes ran up the wall and onto the ceiling; over the end of the beds the outer stripes turned through ninety degrees to form a mitred frame, *and* continued towards the window. There were black-and-white striped curtains and bedspreads, decorated with squares of ultramarine silk edged with emerald green. The bell-like lampshades were of blue silk edged with pink. The oak furniture was simple and rectilinear, and decorated with strips of little blue squares. All this was Viennese in inspiration. The stripes came from Hoffmann, the furniture decorated with squares from Hans Ofner and Otto Prutscher.[10]

There were no triangles here. It was a room of balance and resolutions. The powerful stripes were overlaid with patches of colour

153

178

which Thomas Howarth, who liked to keep Mackintosh masculine, attributed to Margaret. The delicate Viennese squares, self-consciously 'applied' on a raised black strip, left the furniture at once sober and luxurious. Mackintosh had not designed so convincing a bedroom since The Hill House, chiefly because his imagination had fed so much since then on masculine themes of geometry and black. Now he could comprehend both gender poles in one design. In this, his last decorative work of any substance, masculine and feminine, black and white, structure and decoration, Bassett-Lowke and Mackintosh, were in equipoise. Is it churlish to point out, at this moment of triumph, that the one person forgotten was the sleepless guest, staring at those migraine-inducing stripes? When Bassett-Lowke ushered George Bernard Shaw into the room and said 'I trust the decor will not disturb your sleep', Shaw replied 'No, I always sleep with my eyes closed.'[11]

On 8 January 1920 a painter called Harold Squire, who was possibly on the fringes of Mackintosh's circle, asked him to design a studio-house at what is now 49 Glebe Place. On 13 February a Chelsea artist-decorator called Arthur Blunt asked for one at 48 Glebe Place. And at about the same time the sculptor Francis Derwent Wood, who had taught at Glasgow School of Art in the 1890s and was now Professor at the Royal College of Art, asked him to design a studio and workshop at 50 Glebe Place, with lettable artists' studios above. Mackintosh, sensing the longed-for revival of his architectural career, went out and bought Rivington's *Notes on Building Construction* and a copy of Banister Fletcher on *The London Building Acts*. We know this because his office diary for 1920 survives, with notes of professional engagements, and a careful record of expenditure.

Glebe Place is L-shaped. It runs south off the King's Road with late 19th-century houses and studios on either side, and then turns westwards for a narrow stretch, lined with humbler, Georgian buildings on the south and early Victorian stucco on the north. The Mackintoshes' studios were among the humble ones. Where the road turned, you could glimpse an acre of overgrown garden crowded with incongruous statues. On one side of it was Cheyne House, a modest and by then almost completely dilapidated 18th-century building. In the other corner was a brand new, four-storey house encrusted with Venetian-looking balconies and busts of the Royal Family, and known as the 'Mystery House'. All this was the work, or perhaps the play, of the eccentric architect and scientist Dr John Samuel Phené. Phené died in 1912 and in July 1914 his property was advertised for sale in

155

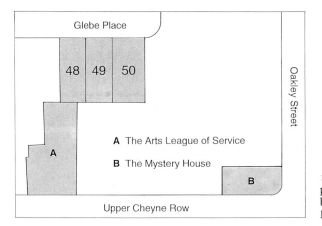

Glebe Place

48 49 50

A

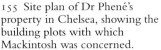

A The Arts League of Service

B The Mystery House

B

Upper Cheyne Row

155 Site plan of Dr Phené's property in Chelsea, showing the building plots with which Mackintosh was concerned.

lots as having 'the strongest appeal to the artist and litterateur'.[12] It may not have sold at that difficult time, but things presumably began to move again after the war, leading to Mackintosh's commissions.

Mackintosh's first idea for Squire was probably to put a tiny gabled building in front with an enormous cat-slide roof, and a two-storey studio building behind, its huge window framed by reveals of stepped brickwork and a roof-top balustrade. The later drawing 'Three Chelsea Studios' shows a version of this. (The building plots were on the south side of Glebe Place, so a north-facing studio window had to be part of the street front.) Then, possibly in March, he dropped the little building, made the studio window smaller and brought the main block up to the street, a blunter arrangement. Either way, this front was the most up-to-date of Mackintosh's designs, the grid of the window and the stepped architrave echoing Vienna (Hoffmann regarded the stepped architrave as his invention) and perhaps also Dutch Expressionist architecture.

Blunt cannot have needed a north-facing studio window, for he got a Georgian-ish three-bay design, not so different from modest 18th-century houses in Chelsea. For Wood Mackintosh designed a large, rather bare building in the farmhouse vernacular favoured by Arts and Crafts architects before the war, with big studio windows. It seems that he was still fascinated by the square, and therefore content with the minimal formula of roughcast and glazing bars, as he had been at Windyhill and The Hill House. The ground landlord for all Dr Phené's property was the Glebe of Chelsea, a church body. When Mackintosh submitted the Wood elevations to their surveyor for approval, he was told they needed 'more architectural qualities'.[13]

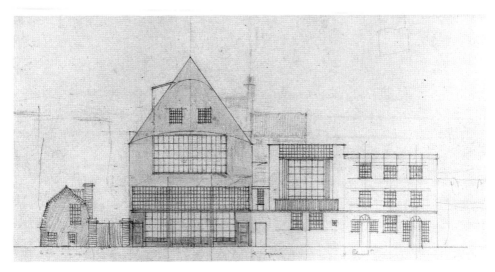

156 Detail of designs for studios for Francis Derwent Wood (left) and studio-houses for Harold Squire (middle) and Arthur Blunt (right) in Glebe Place, London, probably February–June 1920. Pencil, ink and watercolour with crayon on brown tracing paper.

157 'Block of Studios: Cheyne House Chelsea'. Designs for studios and studio-flats on the site of Cheyne House, May 1920 or later. Pencil and watercolour.

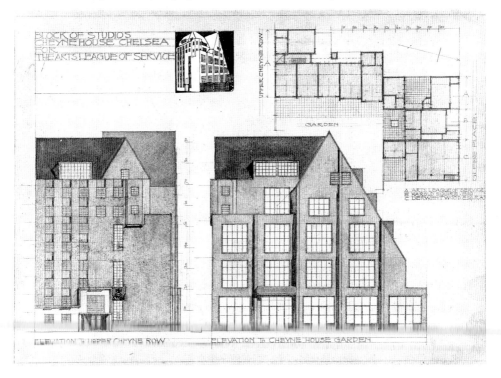

Towards the end of March 1920 Mackintosh looked over the bizarre Mystery House with J. D. Fergusson, Margaret Morris and a round, energetic Chilean woman called Ana Berry, who ran the Arts League of Service. The League was set up in 1919 'To Bring the Arts into Everyday Life'. A travelling theatre was one arm of its endeavours, craft and design another – artists working on everyday things. Fergusson, Goossens and Schwabe were all involved in it, and the thought was that it might take over the Mystery House; Mackintosh did a scheme for this. At the other end of the garden, Cheyne House had been demolished, and late in March Miss Berry asked Mackintosh what she should offer for that site. He said £1,850, and she asked him to design a block of studios and flats for it. She was thinking of a co-operative scheme, with artist-tenants taking shares in the property – another way to help the arts.

157 Mackintosh designed a gabled block in two parts: there were four studio-flats on the west side, with living accommodation on mezzanines, giving vertical strips of windows overlooking Upper Cheyne Row, and nineteen studios on the east side, with a great wall of windows looking out over the garden. Mackintosh put as much accommodation as he could on the site: the height of the building and the slope of the roof on the north side were both the maximum allowed by the London Building Act of 1894. And the height and mass brought Scotland to his mind. The stepping-back of the garden front and the chamfered, overhanging corner of the fourth floor are stylized versions of details on 17th-century tenements in Edinburgh, while the two principal fronts of the building, one all studio windows, the other all vertical strips, recall his own greatest work in Glasgow. By the end of April the scheme was sufficiently advanced for Mackintosh to get estimates for building in reinforced concrete, and in May he reported on the scheme to the Glebe of Chelsea.

In June Margaret Morris brought a proposal for a theatre, to go somewhere on the Glebe's land, though it is not known where. The 158 design only exists in the form of plans, sections and one elevation, rather drily drawn. It has one of Mackintosh's jazzy architraves jammed between pepper-pot towers, and a plan that recalls his alternative design for a concert hall at the International Exhibition of 1901. But it is hard to imagine what it would have looked like in brick or, more probably, brick and concrete.

Mackintosh must now have blessed the chance that had brought him to Glebe Place five years before. In six months he had been asked to design five separate buildings, all for artists, all on his doorstep, one

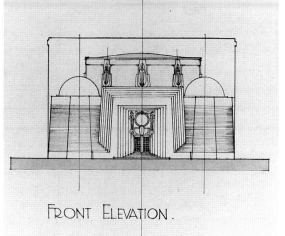

158 Design for a theatre for Margaret Morris. Detail of the front elevation, 1920. Pencil, ink and watercolour.

FRONT ELEVATION.

big and ambitious. Chelsea might be the salvation of his architectural career after all. In a curious way, he seemed to be following in the footsteps of C. R. Ashbee, who had made a success of designing houses for artists in Chelsea before the war. These were sometimes vernacular, sometimes Georgian in style, but always deliberately various, as Mackintosh's were. Ashbee designed big studio-blocks, and he even took hints from Edinburgh tenements. Every time the Mackintoshes went to the Blue Cockatoo they walked past his clever, understated studio-houses at 37–39 Cheyne Walk. Here was an example to be followed.

But designing is one thing, building another. In May 1920 Blunt decided that he wanted timbers from an old barn to be incorporated in his house. Mackintosh redesigned it and wrote to the London County Council about a licence. After that, nothing is known about the scheme. Squire's house was further forward: Mackintosh got estimates on 11 May; the next day Squire asked him to send them to his sister, Mrs Claude, at the Hyde Park Hotel (she seems to have been paying for the work). A month later he came back asking for a cheaper scheme, with all the accommodation on one floor. Mackintosh moved the studio back from the road again, and put a hopeless, blank little single-storey building in front of it, just a brick wall with two doors, two windows and a chimney, and a lean-to roof sloping back from the street. Building started in July, stopped because the Claudes had not yet bought the land, started again in September, and then stopped again to put bedrooms on the roof. It was probably completed some time in 1921. Wood's studio was still on the drawing board; but

183

it was never built. And as for the block of studios, it seems that the Arts League wanted to build on more of the site than their building agreement (presumably with the ground landlord) allowed for, and the scheme had to be dropped.

It may have been in about December that Mackintosh, at whose suggestion we do not know, designed an equally striking and equally Scottish-looking block for the League to go on Blunt's now vacant site. And at this time, or perhaps later, he took two very fetching elevation drawings he had made of the first (January–February) proposals for Wood and Squire, made matching drawings of his new (December) design for the League, and stuck them together. This produced the elevations entitled 'Three Chelsea Studios'. It had been a busy year, architecturally; but all he had to show for it was drawings of schemes that could not be built, and a sad little building in Glebe Place.

The last entry in the office diary is for 13 January 1921. '3 Venus pencils 1/6, 1 bt Chinese ink 1/3, 1 bot writing ink 2d'. After that we know very little for almost three years. Small facts, some important some not, are scattered across the years. In April 1921 Mackintosh exhibited a design for silks at the Friday Club. On 12 December 1921 Frances McNair died in Glasgow, perhaps by her own hand, and her husband, devastated, destroyed most of her work. In 1922 Mackintosh designed a binding for a series of boys' stories by G. A. Henty, published by Walter Blackie. And at about this time Margaret contributed to the project of the Queen's Doll's House with a tiny watercolour of a mother and child.

In December 1922 the 'Three Chelsea Studios' drawings and the companion 'Block of Studios' were included in an 'Exhibition of Contemporary British Architecture' at the Royal Institute of British Architects. The exhibition consisted mainly of pre-war work by leading Edwardians – Ernest Newton, Sir Edwin Lutyens, Mewès and Davis, Sir Edwin Cooper – much of it shown in photographs at the Institute's request. One hopes that Mackintosh did not go, for it can only have made the architect in him feel lonely and out-of-date. Here were the achievements of British architecture before the war, civic, commercial and domestic, captured in the reality of photographs. And all he had to show was drawings of four unexecuted buildings which looked, to one reviewer, as if they had come out of the early volumes of *The Studio*. After this we know nothing, except that at some point in 1923, on the advice of friends, the Mackintoshes set out for a long holiday in the south of France.

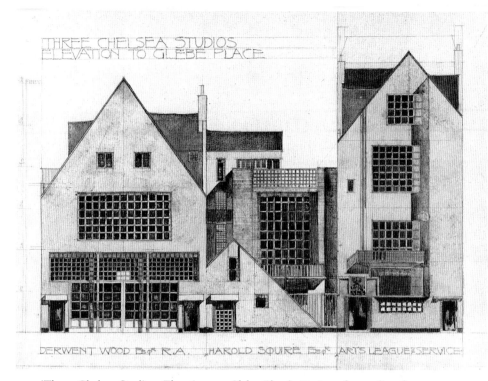

159 'Three Chelsea Studios: Elevation to Glebe Place'. Designs for studios for Francis Derwent Wood (left), a studio-house for Harold Squire (middle) and studios or studio-flats for The Arts League of Service (right) in Glebe Place, London. The designs for Wood and Squire probably date from January–February 1920, that for the Arts League of Service from December 1920 or later. Pencil and watercolour.

The Chelsea years ended as they had begun, on an equivocal note. Mackintosh had not reached the point of giving up as an architect and designer. Letters of 1919 show him searching for work, and 78 Derngate shows that his invention had not failed. But the war and his lack of contacts in London made it an almost impossible task. At the same time, he seemed to be moving on. He cultivated the company of artists. He began to paint seriously himself, as he had not done since the mid-1890s. And his designs for printed textiles, themselves a new departure, were influenced in part by modern painting. Though the Mackintoshes were not at the centre of the avant-garde in London, his Chelsea work only makes sense in the context of avant-garde movements of 1910–14, Post-Impressionism, Vorticism, the Omega

Workshops. And perhaps it was good for Mackintosh to be in touch with these things. Being a modern architect in Glasgow only made him feel lonely. Being a modern artist in Chelsea brought him friends.

As for his personal life, life with Margaret, there are only uncertainties. Looking back over these years, some people remembered the Mackintoshes' amusing tea-parties and sociability; others recalled Mackintosh depressed, turned in upon himself, unable to speak. His work shows that his spirit was not crushed. But what are we to make of the photographs of Mackintosh taken by his friend E. O. Hoppé at about this time? Even allowing for Hoppé's artistic gloom, they are sad. Mackintosh's face has grown big and flat. It is hard to believe that this is the same man as the dapper, expectant figure photographed by Annan in 1893.

160

13

160 Charles Rennie Mackintosh in about 1920, photographed by E. O. Hoppé.

CHAPTER SIX

Love, Work and Peace
Port Vendres 1923–1933

The long holiday turned into four years, spent living in cheap hotels, eating good, simple food and learning about the sun. (In the 1920s a hotel in the south of France would be much cheaper than lodgings in London.) Whatever had been wrong in Chelsea, and before that in Glasgow, seemed to come right by the shores of the Mediterranean. They went as far south as they could, to the southern tip of the Roussillon, with its coastline of fishing villages and the great wall of the Pyrenees standing up over the plain on a clear day. They were alone together, and seem to have moved from place to place. In January 1924 they were in the spa town of Amélie-les-Bains, a sort of Cheltenham-in-the-Pyrenees, and in April perhaps in the port of Collioure, which had been the favourite summer painting resort of the Fauves (Matisse had been coming there since 1905). This may have been their first base. February 1925 found them at Ille-sur-Têt, a grey town in the foothills of the Pyrenees where the food was good and the hotel only cost four shillings a day. Mackintosh wrote to J. D. Fergusson that the workmen sitting at a long table in the dining room reminded him of *The Last Supper*, 'only there is no frugality here and the wine flows in a way that would have given life and gaiety to Leonardo's popular masterpiece'.[1] And in July, perhaps to escape the heat, they were five thousand feet up in Mont Louis, a tiny fortified town on the grassy uplands of the Pyrenees.

The Hôtel du Commerce at Port Vendres was the nearest thing to a home that the Mackintoshes ever had in France; they were there in December 1925. The dining room on the first floor looked across the harbour and out to sea; they kept themselves to themselves – Mackintosh's French was not very good – and the proprietors, M. and Mme Dejean, treated them with that mixture of sympathy, distance and gentle curiosity which hoteliers offer to the permanently uprooted. It was not the obvious place for them to settle. Collioure, about 2 miles (3 kilometres) up the coast, was where artists went. There, the fishermen beached their boats in the shadow of a medieval castle and Matisse thought there was no bluer sky in France. Port

161

Vendres, on the other hand, was not in its 20th-century form particularly old, or particularly pretty. It was a busy modern port whose life was centred on big cargo ships from Algeria, and smaller boats from Spain and Italy bringing beans and wine and wood. There were no artists in Port Vendres; Mackintosh's closest associates, the painters Rudolph Ihlee and Edgar Hereford, lived in Collioure. Perhaps Mackintosh, who was engaged on a new and serious body of work, needed to withdraw a little from the artists' colony. And perhaps, in a small way, the port brought back memories of Glasgow.

In December 1925 he wrote to Francis Newbery: 'I am struggling to paint in watercolour – soon I shall start in oils.'[2] Forty-one watercolours survive from these years, but no oils. They include views of individual farmhouses, flower studies, and four deliberately naive views of cargo boats unloading. But the great majority are landscapes composed of hillsides, rocks, and clustered buildings. They were done wherever the Mackintoshes stayed, twelve of them at Port Vendres. He did not paint the landscape as he found it; he was, as always, governed by his imagination, and was happy to move lighthouses, promontories and mountains to get his composition right. And he liked to combine different viewpoints: the lower part of *Palalda, Pyrénées-Orientales* represents a point of view from the south side of the River Tech, the upper from Route D115 much higher up. He worked slowly, and always out of doors. Mary Sturrock remembered him painting in Walberswick, using Whatman hot-press paper which he literally soaked with colour, working it in with a toothbrush. He probably did the same in France.

Very few of the paintings are dated, and they do not fall into an obvious stylistic sequence. But the majority show a distinctive graphic style: the paper is marked out into distinct areas in pencil, and then worked up with washes of colour, creating layers and planes. The paintings are focused on buildings and rocks, hard, definite and many-sided; the hillsides are generally mere backgrounds. Palalda, a spectacular mediaeval hill-town outside Amélie-les-Bains, becomes a cluster of planes in various perspectives. A group of slightly fissured rocks in the bay at Port Vendres becomes a series of stylized layers. We should not think here of Cézanne and the geometry of nature. Mackintosh was not exploring the landscape or his own perceptions. He was, rather, bringing his talents as a designer to bear upon the landscape.

These watercolours were not just a pastime of retirement; they were both exploration and fulfilment. Their graphic style perhaps betrays

161 Quai Pierre Forgas, Port Vendres, showing the Hôtel du Commerce.

the former architect, but their substance was new: we have scarcely had to use words like 'plane' and 'layer' before. Mackintosh had begun a new career as a painter. At the same time, they were a home-coming. Ever since he walked into Annan's studio to have himself photographed in 1893, he had thought of himself as an artist. The strengths, weaknesses and originality of his work stemmed in part from that. Now, he was an artist. He had arrived, on the shores of the Mediterranean, at the point from which he set out.

The watercolours belong to the end of his life. He and Margaret were outsiders, tourists and artists. Their first relationship was to the landscape, not to the people of the Roussillon. The streets in Mackintosh's paintings are empty, and there is no one in the fields. The houses are not dwellings, but planes and surfaces, formally inter-changeable with rocks. The man-made and the natural landscape have the same rough geometry. The paintings are both an idealization of the vernacular and an expression of not needing people. They are very different from the joyful, sensual landscapes which Matisse painted at Collioure. But they seem to express an austere peace which Mackintosh found in the Roussillon – and perhaps Margaret also, though no paintings survive by her. Their last years were neither empty nor lonely. They were fifty-five and fifty-nine when they came

189

to France, and had suffered a good deal. But they had perhaps reached a time when emptiness and fulfilment are not far apart.

At the beginning of May 1927, Margaret went back to London for medical treatment and was away for almost two months. Mackintosh wrote to her about every other day, keeping his letters until he had covered as many sheets as the cheapest stamp would carry. Margaret kept the letters, and later they passed into the possession of the family of William Davidson, by whom they were given to the University of Glasgow. A condition of the gift, however, was that they should not be published in any way and should only be made available for purposes of research. Here, therefore, they cannot be quoted from.

162 *Palalda, Pyrénées-Orientales, c.* 1924–7. Pencil and watercolour.

163 *The Rocks*, 1927. Pencil and watercolour.

Mackintosh wrote about his daily round, expressing his slow pleasure in ordinary things – the smell and sound of ships loading and
unloading in the harbour, the food at dinner (soup, sole, asparagus,
chicken, Roquefort, cherries – all good), M. Dejean and his family
going out to the cinema, the sea flat and blue with no wind; perhaps
he will walk over to Collioure this evening; a crow has been talking
to him. At first, they gave him a whole bottle of wine at dinner, as if
she were still there; but he tells her proudly that he has left half of it.
Drink, it seems, was no longer a problem.

Margaret could have imagined all or any of this, they had been
together for so long; and that made him feel that he had nothing to
say to her. He need not have worried. His love for her is clear on every

page, clearest of all in the trivialities. Here, right at the end of his life, Mackintosh reveals himself to us, as an ordinary, slightly defeated man, rising sixty, sometimes angry or depressed, often funny, intent on his work, and trying to understand what he feels with his wife so long away.

Running through the letters is the name of Christian Barman of *The Architectural Association Journal*, who wanted to do an article about Mackintosh's work in Glasgow. Mackintosh was becoming famous again. In 1924 Charles Marriott, the architecture critic of *The Times*, published a broad, representative survey entitled *Modern English Architecture* and wrote of Mackintosh, almost in passing, 'It is hardly too much to say that the whole modernist movement in European architecture derives from him'.[3] Barman also wanted Mackintosh to write several articles about contemporary English architecture, but Mackintosh replied gruffly that he couldn't because it didn't exist. As he enjoyed the healthy life and simple routines of their Mediterranean retreat, architecture seemed to him a world away, something he had left behind. It made him think of big cities and professional careers, and the only note of anger in his letters comes from these things, as he spits and swears against a modern America which serves the mass and not the individual, or against Charles Reilly, Professor of Architecture at Liverpool University, for whom he nursed a bitter and unexplained hatred.

163 He was painting *The Rocks* at this time, and we can watch him at work. On 16 May he has painted the houses in the background and must start on the rocks themselves; it scares him. Two days later he has had a wonderful time with sun and no wind and he has mastered the drawing of the rocks; now it will do as he wants. On 24 May the weather was perfect – if there was wind it shook the cardboard on which he mounted his work. By 27 May he has almost finished and he seems to have got rid of the green in his palette which he regards as a curse, a colour he puts in almost without thinking. Two days later he is sad to think that when he has finished work he will not see Margaret coming to greet him, bounding over the hill like a chamois. On 31 May he tells her that she can throw away his top hat and tail coat. He will not need them any more. Meanwhile, he would keep his watercolours private; he would not have them seen in an exhibition until, different though they were, they could hold their own beside other people's work.

Early in the letters, Mackintosh mentioned that his tongue was swollen, and blamed it on the American tobacco which was all he could get. In fact he had cancer of the tongue, for he had been a smoker all his life. In the autumn of 1927 he became seriously ill and Rudolph Ihlee took him back to London. Jessie Newbery met them at the station and took him to Westminster Hospital where he was given radium treatment. He came out of hospital after a few months, unable to speak. He wanted to sit under a tree, so Margaret rented rooms in Willow Road, Hampstead, with a tree in the garden. Margaret Morris gave him exercises to get his voice back, and then, when he finally could not speak at all, she just held his hand and helped him to make signs. Later the Mackintoshes moved from Willow Road to a friend's house in Porchester Square, Paddington; and in the autumn of 1928 Mackintosh went into a nursing home. He died there on 10 December 1928. The funeral was held the next day at Golders Green Crematorium.

Margaret, alone, took to a wandering life again. She moved from hotel to hotel, anxious about her health. By December she was back in the Hôtel du Commerce. In 1929 she tried to organize an exhibition of her husband's work, but nothing came of it. That summer she took a cure in Normandy. And she must have gone to the Hôtel du Commerce again for the Ihlees dined with her on several occasions. 'I really came to know her after her husband's death', Mme Ihlee recalled, 'and I remember thinking, all those years ago, that she never talked about him.'[4] January 1932 found her in a hotel in Falmouth, and then she was in Harrogate for another cure. All this time they had kept on Mackintosh's studio in Glebe Place; furniture, watercolours and hundreds of drawings from the Glasgow days were stored there. In December 1932 Margaret came back to Chelsea, but she only lived a few more weeks, and died in a nursing home on 7 January 1933.

After the cremation, Randolph Schwabe wrote to her brother and executor Archibald Macdonald, offering to help sort out her property. 'We are near at hand here, and I know that Margaret was concerned as to certain pictures of Mackintosh and certain pieces of furniture designed by him. The proper place for all these is in some Museum. For those interested in such things Mackintosh as a designer and artist, is an historical figure, and his work should be preserved from dispersal and obscurity.'[5]

CHAPTER SEVEN

Critical Fortunes

Four months later, in May 1933, the drawings, watercolours and furniture left at Margaret's death formed the nucleus of a Memorial
164 Exhibition in Glasgow, organized by William Davidson and Jeffrey Waddell, a Glasgow architect. A review-article in *The Listener* hailed Mackintosh as 'this pioneer of the modern movement in architecture'.[1] Shortly after that, the Mackintosh furniture from Hous'hill was auctioned. Only two people knew what they were buying, and part of a revolving bookcase now in the Scottish National Gallery of Modern Art was mistaken for a wireless aerial.

Mackintosh's reputation had reached a curious point. The people of Glasgow had more or less forgotten him. John Summerson recalled that in the 1920s Mackintosh's works were remembered in Glasgow 'if at all, only as something quite out-moded, and not worth a thought or glance'.[2] But journalists and architects of the new Modernism had discovered him. For architect-writers like the German Bruno Taut and the Australian-born Raymond McGrath, and for Scottish architects like Robert Hurd, whose Modernism derived from the simple masses of the national vernacular, he was a pioneer.

But he did not fit easily into the Modernists' canon. They wanted to see him as an architect concerned with structure and space, and usually dismissed the decorative work as trivial and dated. Thus, in 1933, the critic Philip Morton Shand urged that the Memorial Exhibition should not reflect what he thought of as Margaret's 'rather thin Aubrey Beardsley mannerism of the arty-crafty type'.[3] But Shand knew enough history to see that Mackintosh was 'far less of a constructor than a decorator', and that the role of functionalist pioneer had been thrust upon him.[4] In *Pioneers of the Modern Movement* (1936) Nikolaus Pevsner gave an orthodox Modernist view of Mackintosh as a master in the handling of space and said nothing about the decorative work. In the United States, on the other hand, where the Modernist canon was shaped by the trio of Henry-Russell Hitchcock, Alfred Barr and Philip Johnson, Mackintosh did not win pioneer status at all. Hitchcock thought he was not of prime importance.

164 A view of the Mackintosh Memorial Exhibition in Glasgow Corporation's McLellan Galleries, Sauchiehall Street, May 1933. The immensely tall chair on the left may have been made for Miss Cranston's Tea Rooms in Ingram Street in 1909.

In 1939 a young architect called Thomas Howarth came from Manchester University to teach at Glasgow School of Architecture, and became interested in Mackintosh. He interviewed anyone who remembered him, sorted out the drawings now stored in William Davidson's city warehouse, and registered for a PhD at the University of Glasgow. Davidson was also looking after 6 Florentine Terrace, which he had bought from the Mackintoshes in 1920. When he died in 1945 the house was bought by the University of Glasgow, and his family presented the Mackintosh contents to the University. At the same time the Mackintoshes' heir, Sylvan McNair, renounced his claim to their estate, including the drawings, watercolours and furniture, in favour of the University. This laid the foundations for the principal Mackintosh collection and archive. In 1949 Howarth, who had by then returned to teach at Manchester University, completed his thesis on Mackintosh.

As early as 1934, Pevsner had been working on a book about Mackintosh, but had failed to find a publisher. In 1948 the Italian publishers Il Balcone asked him to write a short account in a series on architects of the Modern Movement. He then wrote to Howarth with a tentative suggestion that they might co-operate on a larger book. Howarth demurred, which may be a pity, for Pevsner's treatment of the decorative work in the little Italian book, published in 1950, was far more perceptive than the party line he followed in *Pioneers*. 'In order to understand Mackintosh,' he wrote, 'it is essential to grasp the fusion in his art of puritanism with sensuality. The enchanting curves of Art Nouveau have the same importance as the austere verticals of the incipient Modern Movement.'[5] (The dualism Modernism/Art Nouveau recalls that of male/female in Muthesius's article of 1902.) Later editions of *Pioneers* were revised to give the structural and the decorative equal weight.

In 1952 Thomas Howarth published *Charles Rennie Mackintosh and the Modern Movement* and it has become the standard work. Howarth was a tenacious researcher, and his interviews made the book an invaluable (if uncheckable) record. He saw Mackintosh as a lonely genius struggling to break the bonds that tied architecture to convention and the past, and his work as rooted in Scottish traditions yet anticipating 20th-century functionalism. He saw 'functional simplicity' in the north front of Glasgow School of Art, and an attempt at 'an architecture of clean-cut mechanical precision' in the façade of the Willow Tea Rooms.[6] But the decorative work made him uneasy. In the School of Art library he was happy to find that 'there are no elongated females, no beads and wire . . . the structural form is emphasized, the lines are dynamic and masculine, and the architect's preoccupation with the manipulation and control of space is everywhere apparent.'[7] Howarth's book lent the authority of an apparently definitive biography to the Modernist interpretation of Mackintosh.

Though Howarth was ahead of his time in researching this period so thoroughly, his argument belonged absolutely to the 1940s and 1950s, when Modernism occupied the mainstream of British architecture. The pleasure of looking at Victorian and Edwardian architecture and design without a Modernist perspective was known to only a few in the 1950s. In 1952 the Victoria and Albert Museum's extraordinarily prescient exhibition 'Victorian and Edwardian Decorative Arts' included Mackintosh not as a lonely genius but as one among many named designers. And then people began to discover Art Nouveau, starting with a big exhibition at the Museum of Modern

Art in New York in 1960 and another in Paris in 1960–61, 'Les Sources du XXe Siècle: Les Arts en Europe de 1884–1914'. At Paris the architecture and decorative arts section was introduced by Pevsner and rich in Art Nouveau, and Mackintosh had the largest single exhibit. For Pevsner, Art Nouveau was a decorative episode of the years round 1900, a style which turned away from the past more decisively than it reached towards the (Modernist) future. Though Mackintosh's straight lines made as little sense alongside the rich curves of French and Belgian Art Nouveau as did those of the Viennese, this context made more historical sense of him than Modernism had. His decorative work could now be understood alongside the structural, and in his own time. In the growing enthusiasm for Art Nouveau in the 1960s, Mackintosh found a prominent place.

Mackintosh's centenary fell in 1968, and Andrew McLaren Young, Professor of Fine Art at the University of Glasgow, organized a big exhibition which was shown in Edinburgh and London, and in a reduced version in Zurich, Darmstadt and Vienna, though not in Glasgow. McLaren Young's approach was catholic: 'Any understanding of him . . . must reconcile the *fin-de-siècle* and the prophetically modern aspects of his work.'[8] But Robert Macleod, in his lucid *Charles Rennie Mackintosh* (1968), challenged the Modernist assumption that Mackintosh belonged to their club. Drawing on Mackintosh's lecture notes and architectural work, Macleod argued that Mackintosh did not emerge 'out of context, out of time'.[9] He belonged to a British tradition of progressive architectural thought which went back to Pugin and the 1830s, a tradition which valued function and modernity, but did not need to cut itself off from the past.

While the critics and historians were debating, Mackintosh seemed to be fading from the fabric of Glasgow. For most Glaswegians, Mackintosh meant the tea rooms he had designed for Miss Cranston, and by the early 1970s they had almost all gone. Buchanan Street and Argyle Street went in about 1918. Ingram Street was Glaswegians' strongest link with Mackintosh, but that ceased to be a tea room in 1950. Glasgow Corporation bought it to save it from destruction, but in 1971 the fittings had to be removed and stored. The Willow, part of Daly's department store since 1927 and much altered, was now threatened by Daly's closure. In 1963 the University demolished 6 Florentine Terrace, storing the fittings for re-erection. Glasgow's urban motorway threatened Martyrs' Public School, and depopulated the catchment area of Scotland Street School. And a shrinking congregation threatened Queen's Cross Church with redundancy.

Mackintosh did not have many advocates in Glasgow at this time. The Friends of Toshie was an important early group; the New Glasgow Society lobbied on his behalf; and the Charles Rennie Mackintosh Society was founded in Glasgow in 1973. Just over twenty years later, the Ingram Street interiors are being reconstructed by Glasgow Museums. The Willow has been carefully restored. The interiors from 6 Florentine Terrace have been meticulously reconstructed as The Mackintosh House, attached to the University's Hunterian Art Gallery. Martyrs' Public School is secure. Scotland Street School is a regional museum of education. And Queen's Cross Church is lovingly cared for as the headquarters of the Mackintosh Society. These things are due to large forces, to inner city renewal, the shift to conservation in city planning, and Glasgow's own 'Renaissance'. But the advocacy of the Mackintosh Society runs through them all.

Buildings saved from demolition and carefully refurbished are only part of the extraordinary drama of Mackintosh's burgeoning reputation since the 1970s, a drama in which the city of Glasgow itself has been both stage and principal actor. Before the 1970s the people who

165 Facsimiles of Mackintosh chairs at the Milan Triennale, 1973, made under the supervision of Filippo Alison of the University of Naples. Professor Alison's work provided prototypes for the range of reproduction Mackintosh furniture manufactured by Cassina and launched at the Milan Triennale.

166 'Mockintosh': mirror-frames, mugs and clocks.

cared about Mackintosh were mainly academics, conservationists, architects with a sense of history, and museum curators, professional people who did not stand to make much money out of him. And many Glaswegians had never even heard of him. Then people started making reproduction Mackintosh furniture: the best-known series, by Cassina of Milan, was launched in 1973. Genuine Mackintosh chairs started breaking records at auction: the first was at Sotheby's on 13 March 1975. Letraset produced a standardized version of Mackintosh lettering, which got everywhere. And someone coined the phrase 'Mockintosh' for a whole range of giftware which used or abused his designs. There were mugs and T-shirts of course. But it is a special feature of the Mockintosh industry that it adapts his designs to objects like jewellery and mirror-frames which he might have designed but actually never, or hardly ever, did. Some people buy these as acceptable substitutes, others buy them as the real thing. Nowadays the people who care about Mackintosh include manufacturers and retailers, auction houses, media people and the people in charge of promotion at Glasgow City Council, who have found in Mackintosh (and the Burrell Collection) the perfect tourist package for Glasgow, new, clean and artistic. A lot of money is at stake. And everyone in Glasgow knows about Mackintosh.

So far as Mackintosh's reputation is concerned, there has been a parting of the ways. The academics and experts have carried on, looking at this aspect of Mackintosh and that, presenting one inter-pretation, then another. (For people professedly in search of truth, we blunder about rather.) But almost everyone else has charged off, waving their mugs and mirror-frames, into a kind of Mackintosh theme park, full of stereotypes, money-making and people having fun. We shall stay with the academics for the moment.

One important development of the 1970s was that the study of Mackintosh's furniture was put on a scholarly basis. The Mackintosh literature has always been richer in interpretation than in the schol-arly sifting of facts. Thomas Howarth and the Scottish architectural historian David Walker have sorted much of the architectural work, and Andrew McLaren Young, a man of considerable vision, brought the University of Glasgow's collection into a scholarly and disciplined shape. But McLaren Young died in 1975, walking up the steps of the Royal Academy. His work at the University was continued by his assistant, Roger Billcliffe, whose massive and intricate catalogue raisonné, *Charles Rennie Mackintosh: The Complete Furniture, Furniture Drawings & Interior Designs* (1979) has laid the proper foundations for research. Billcliffe has an appetite for discoveries and completeness, and the thoroughness of this and his other summary catalogues has put all later writers, collectors and curators in his debt.

In 1983 the Mackintosh Society organized a conference entitled 'Mackintosh: National and International'. There were papers on Muthesius, Frank Lloyd Wright, Greene and Greene, Olbrich, Ödön Lechner, Hector Guimard, Antoní Gaudí, Viennese furniture and several British architects. The idea behind the conference was that Mackintosh was one of a handful of architects and designers in Europe and America at the turn of the century who drew inspiration for their modernism from national or regional vernaculars; and that there may have been something like an international style before the Bauhaus, with Mackintosh as its catalyst. This was perfectly expressed by an American woman whom I once overheard in The Mackintosh House, explaining to her daughter, 'Yes, dear, this is the architect's own house, and if it had been in our country, he would have been Frank Lloyd Wright.'

It is an attractive idea. Like Modernism, it gives Mackintosh heroic status, and like the 1960s enthusiasm for Art Nouveau, it allows his work to be seen as a whole and in its own time. But the papers, published in 1988 as *Mackintosh & His Contemporaries in Europe and America*, suggest that it does not work. Though uneven in quality, they show that Wright, Greene and Greene, Lechner, Guimard and Gaudí all differed so much from each other and from Mackintosh in their work that there can have been no common purpose or shared achievement among them. What is more, they throw almost no light on Mackintosh himself.

The two most recent books on Mackintosh deal with his symbolism. In *C. R. Mackintosh: The Poetics of Workmanship* (1992) David Brett showed Mackintosh's symbolic imagination flowering in buildings and interiors of the early 1900s designed around a male/female polarity: the exteriors rough, structurally expressive, masculine, the interiors increasingly smooth, structurally disguised and feminine. For Brett, the feminine interior is a 'centre of spiritual innovation fired by an idealised erotic imagery', and that innovation is the heart of Mackintosh's modernism.[10] Timothy Neat's *Part Seen, Part Imagined* (1994), a much clumsier work, argues that Mackintosh and Margaret were artist-lovers on the highest sexual and spiritual plane, and that the story of their love is told in their symbolic watercolours. The esoteric imagery of these works has baffled earlier writers, but Neat has a sharp eye, a head stuffed with traditional symbols, and a powerful imagination. His account of the symbolic watercolours is plausible, and wholly unverified. I have plundered Brett and Neat for insights which would otherwise have escaped my too-sceptical mind; but in the end I prefer my down-to-earth Mackintosh to Brett's feminist wizard or Neat's lover-genius.

And what of the theme park? What is the state of Mackintosh's popular reputation? While studying the furniture and interiors in The Mackintosh House, I got into the habit of jotting down the remarks of visitors which I overheard. Those notes are the best evidence I have of how people see Mackintosh, so here is a selection, in the order in which I heard them: 'It's end of 19th century, early 20th, but there's something so contemporary about it.' Small Glaswegian boy: 'Why is it all white, Dad?' Dad: 'Because the man was a genius.' 'All the wood was dark [in Victorian times] and he came and painted it all white.' 'He died penniless.' 'It must have been terribly modern at the time. Lovely lamps.' 'When you think what people's houses were like at the time, so crammed. These places are so restful, empty.'

There are two images here: the pioneer who leads us out of the darkness of the 19th century into the light of the 20th, and the genius who dies penniless and misunderstood. (The Japanese cartoon magazine *Young Jump* runs a series called 'Geniuses without Glory', in which the Mackintoshes recently figured.) We have met this version of Mackintosh before. It is not what I have called 'the Mackintosh myth', which is a misconstruction of details in Mackintosh's career. It is a much larger construction of Mackintosh which the myth supports, and we have met it in the standard work by Thomas Howarth. Howarth's book and the popular image of Mackintosh are both informed by stereotypes of the genius, rooted in 19th-century Romanticism, and of the pioneer, rooted in 20th-century progressivism. Howarth's Modernist version of Mackintosh may have lost academic credibility, but it lives on in the popular imagination.

I have drawn a very different picture of Mackintosh in this book. I have not called him a genius because I am not sure what it means. And I have not called him a pioneer because his work did not look forward to Modernism, though one can see why the Modernists looked back to him. He was an ordinary, hard-working man with extraordinary talents, and he did not always know where he was going.

167 A page from Morita Shingo's 'Geniuses without Glory: New Series, 8: C. R. Mackintosh, The Architect Ahead of His Time' *Young Jump*, vol. 2, *c.* 1993. In the top frame, a thick-necked John Keppie says to Mackintosh: 'Your work is too novel. No clients will touch you.' Bottom right: 'He was famous abroad but still overlooked at home. Mackintosh indulged in drink.' Then Margaret murmurs 'My dear . . . We have only a few allies in Glasgow.'

As an architect he started as an exponent of the Free Style with clever mouldings and a penchant for playing games. Free Style architects were often witty, but some of Mackintosh's games were unusual – the flaunting of merely apparent construction, making faces, playing in the gap between plan and elevation, and most of all the difficult games of discontinuity and contradiction which he played, notably at the School of Art. When he used harling round 1900, his formal language changed from mouldings to masses; but the games went on – The Hill House is a plain white box filled with a controlled and sumptuous aestheticism. And when he returned to stone and mouldings, he produced two of his greatest buildings, Scotland Street School and the west wing of the School of Art, not because the materials suited him better, but because he did not have an indulgent client: he had something to fight against.

As a decorative artist Mackintosh spent the 1890s exploring furniture, posters, mural decoration and interiors. It is not until the Mains Street flat that we feel the power of a collaboration which carried the domestic interior deeper into the realm of personal psychology than any comparable contemporary work. These collaborative interiors, with their cloistered atmosphere and symbolic details, could not be more different from the bare cliffs of the School of Art, but they were as great an achievement. I have guessed, however, that the collaboration did not last long. The Hous'hill interior was cooler, more rational. After Hous'hill came the late tea rooms and the Derngate interiors, where Mackintosh adopted a dense and keyed-up treatment of Viennese motifs appropriate to places of entertainment, but innocent of personal or symbolic meaning.

As a designer of furniture, Mackintosh has had short shrift in this book, for it has been possible to illustrate only a tiny proportion of the hundreds of pieces he designed. Most of his furniture was designed for particular rooms, of which he was often also the designer, and we have seen the kind of formal control which he exercised. Move a Mackintosh chair in a Mackintosh interior, one might almost say, and you alter the whole ensemble. But there was formal experiment as well as formal control. For Mackintosh the image of a piece of furniture mattered more than traditional good sense, construction or comfort. As a result his furniture, though made for particular settings, survives quite well outside them. In recent years some of his most striking designs have been lifted from their original settings, manufactured in quantity, placed under the photographer's lights, and transformed into 'design classics' with great success. In 1974 a

165

selection of facsimile Mackintosh chairs went on show at the Museum of Modern Art in New York, and the critic Ada Louise Huxtable wrote: 'The chairs of Charles Rennie Mackintosh are spectral. They are presences. They upstage people. They have more strength and identity than anyone in a room.'[11]

When I started work on Mackintosh I thought it would be important to study him in context; and by that I meant the immediate context of British architecture and design round 1900. I have not done that. I have found Mackintosh to be a lonely figure who drew so heavily on his own formal imagination that much of what was going on around him was irrelevant. We have seen how he drew inspiration from the English Free Style, from Scottish vernacular and from Vienna, but none of these influences went to the heart of his work. The discontinuity, the interiors which express both spirituality and sensuality, were all his own, and Margaret's.

And just as he only took a little from his British contemporaries, so they only took a little from him. In Glasgow one can see the influence of his mouldings on buildings of the early 1900s. His white interiors may have given a clearer direction to the Glasgow Style. And Gourock Central Senior School outside Glasgow (1908) was rather clumsily modelled on Scotland Street School. But that is all. Of buildings in England influenced by Mackintosh, I only know of the Fighting Cocks public house in Moseley, Birmingham (1898–99), whose tower was partly modelled on that of the *Glasgow Herald* building. We have already guessed at the extent of Mackintosh's influence in Europe and America. Research will enlarge our sense of his influence in Britain, but it is unlikely to transform it.

Where then did he stand? If the Mackintosh myth is a myth, what is his historical importance? There are two answers to this. The first is that his historical importance is much like that which Pevsner gave to Art Nouveau: his work belonged to the years round 1900; it challenged what Pevsner called the historicism of the 19th century; its decorative aspects were more influential than the architectural; it excited, among others, European architects and designers who would play a part in the development of Modernism; and it was quickly over. The second answer is that it does not matter. Mackintosh is important for what he designed, not for what others may have designed because of him.

His achievement can be summed up in three words. The first is intellect. I do not mean that Mackintosh's work was shaped to any great degree by intellectual convictions which can be expressed in words, though both Howarth and Macleod in different ways thought that it was. I mean that Mackintosh designed, not just with stone and plaster, or forms and masses, but with thoughts and perceptions. And they were not his thoughts and perceptions but ours. The games he played are all about what we think. They show a sophistication unequalled among his British contemporaries. And the most dangerous game, discontinuity, brings the highest rewards: Mackintosh made his designs loose, open, ready to collapse, because he was inviting us to intervene and, in our minds, hold them up. If intellectuals are clever people who experience the world as thought, and if you can be an intellectual in stone and wood rather than words, Mackintosh was an intellectual.

The second is originality. Mackintosh's buildings, interiors and furniture were often astonishingly novel. He did not take the dark Victorian world and paint it white, as visitors to The Mackintosh House sometimes suppose; the white interiors were based on late Victorian convention. But the Mains Street drawing room was more spare, more rectilinear and more controlled than any contemporary interior in Britain. And this is only to speak in stylistic terms. If David Brett is right, these stylistic features served to create a new and liberating kind of domesticity, instinct with sexuality, a project of a much more profoundly original kind.

The third is inventiveness. He was like a spring, a constant source of new designs. We see this in the variety of surface and motif on Queen's Cross Church, in the intricate, open, three-dimensional sculpture which is what his furniture sometimes seems to be, and in the story of his creative life. During the years of collaboration with Margaret, particularly, new designs seemed to come spiralling out of him in a flood. Something happened after that, some check. But we should not forget the later works, different though they are from the works of his prime. The interiors at Derngate, the watercolours in the south of France are all the more impressive for the fact that they come, creatively, out of almost nothing.

There were limits to his talents. He designed interiors which in their intensity seemed to refuse the variety and vitality of ordinary life. He designed furniture which we praise as sculpture, but which sometimes fails to meet the most basic requirements of comfort or construction. There is arrogance in that. (On the whole, his buildings work better: we have seen how Walter Blackie enjoyed The Hill House, and the School of Art goes on working as a school of art and giving pleasure to its users.) And by standing apart, hugging his identity as an artist, he did not share in the richness of British architecture at the turn of the century: the intelligent preoccupation of the Arts and Crafts movement with sound workmanship and ordinary life, the creative worldliness of an architect like Norman Shaw whose buildings dramatize his clients' aspirations more than his own, the richness of traditional meanings in domestic architecture, the simple and terrible message expressed in the monuments of the First World War. These things were not exceptional. They were typical of British architecture at the turn of the century, and Mackintosh could have shared in them.

And yet there is such a strange power in his work. When I was researching this book in Glasgow, I would often spend my Sunday mornings outside the School of Art, studying its complexities. And Glaswegians would come with their weekend guests and explain to them why the building was important. They have not always done that, it is true, and their view of him is often stereotyped. But there is something real and moving in Glaswegians' affection for Mackintosh. The distinctiveness of his work and its apparent modernity appeal to them. Sometimes I would be tempted to say: 'Look, that doesn't make sense historically.' But to have intervened would be to forget that there was already a conversation going on. Mackintosh was talking to them, speaking through his building.

Looking back over the development of Mackintosh's reputation, I reflect that this book comes at the end of the story, and I wonder whether it will enjoy some brief authority as a conclusion. But I know that part of Mackintosh's inventiveness is that he is able to reinvent himself. He was whatever he was during his lifetime. Then he became a Modernist, then a master of Art Nouveau, then a pioneer of liberated sexuality. I expect people will say that I have made him into a Postmodernist, though I did not set out to do that. At all events, I am sure that this will not be the last word.

Notes

Abbreviations:

GSA Glasgow School of Art
HAG The Hunterian Art Gallery,
     University of Glasgow
SRA Strathclyde Regional Archives,
     Mitchell Library, Glasgow

Sources listed in the bibliography are referred to in the notes in shortened form: e.g., Jones 1990 = Anthony Jones, *Charles Rennie Mackintosh*, London and Edison, N. J., 1990

Foreword (pp. 7–8)
1 Letter of 16 May 1927 (HAG).

Chapter One (pp. 9–18)
1 Robertson 1990, p. 51.
2 ibid., p. 50.
3 ibid., pp. 91, 94.
4 ibid., p. 101.

Chapter Two (pp. 19–65)
1 *British Architect*, 22 Jan. and 4 Mar. 1892 (the chapter house); 8 July and 26 Aug. 1892 (the Art Gallery); 24 Feb. 1893 (the railway terminus).
2 Robertson 1990, p. 207.
3 Howarth 1990, p. 19.
4 *Builder*, 20 May 1893.
5 *Quiz*, 15 Nov. 1894; *Bailie*, 14 Nov. 1894; *Glasgow Evening News*, 13 Nov. 1894.
6 *Glasgow Evening News*, 1 Feb. 1895.
7 Howarth 1990, p. 32.
8 Voysey's 'Studios for a London Street' were published in *Builder*, 2 Dec. 1892.
9 Howarth 1990, pp. 38–39. See also Jones 1990, p. 33: 'Their work was pounced upon by the critics and the public and subjected to a loud chorus of disapproval.'
10 *Studio*, vol. 9, 1896, pp. 203-4.
11 ibid.
12 *Builder*, 17 Oct. 1896, p. 301.
13 In 1899 and 1916. For a full discussion of this episode, see Helland 1994.
14 Howarth 1990, p. 79.
15 *Dekorative Kunst*, vol. 1, 1897, p. 50.
16 Mackintosh to Muthesius, 2 and 18 Nov. 1897 (HAG); *Dekorative Kunst*, vol. 3, 1898, pp. 48–49 and illustrations on pp. 69-76.
17 Muthesius 1902, p. 208.
18 This work has until recently been dated to 1897, following Howarth 1990, p. 124. However, the archives of the Dean of Guild (SRA) and the *Glasgow Advertiser and Property Circular* for 20 Oct. 1899 show that that the

major refurbishment of the Argyle Street premises, including Walton's decorative work, took place between June 1898 and Sept. 1899. It is likely that Mackintosh's furniture dates from this period, especially as Howarth 1990, p. 124, states that Francis Smith, cabinet-maker, sent furniture designed by Mackintosh to Argyle Street in 1898 and 1899.
19 Savage 1980, p. 68.
20 Information on technical aspects of Mackintosh's furniture from Brian McKerracher, conservator at the HAG.
21 Buchanan 1989, pp. 36-37.
22 Letter of 11 May 1898 (HAG).
23 Muthesius 1979, p. 124.
24 *Builders' Journal*, 18 June 1895, p. 301, of the *Glasgow Herald* building.
25 Nuttgens 1988, p. 74.
26 Letter of 18 Nov. 1897 (HAG).
27 Moffat 1989, p. 23.

Chapter Three (pp. 66–139)
1 Muthesius 1902, p. 215.
2 Brett 1988, p. 6.
3 Muthesius 1979, pp. 51-52.
4 ibid., p. 51.
5 In *De la Tamise à la Sprée*, Reims 1905, quoted in Howarth 1990, p. 46.
6 Bedford and Davies 1973, p. 281.
7 Schweiger 1984, p. 17.
8 Howarth 1990, p. 154. See also Billcliffe 1986, p. 96: 'The exhibition was an enormous critical success for Mackintosh.' And Jones 1990, p. 7: 'His genius hopscotched over England to be recognized in middle Europe where, as the new century dawned, he was worshipped in Vienna for works that were icons, and ideas that were both prescriptions and prophesies.'
9 Howarth 1990, p. 270.
10 See Billcliffe and Vergo 1977, p. 740.
11 *Neues Wiener Tagblatt*, 3 Nov. 1900, quoted in Sekler 1973, p. 136; *Wiener Rundschau*, 1 Dec. 1900, quoted in Howarth 1990, p. 153.
12 *Wiener Allgemeine Zeitung*, 4 Nov. 1900, quoted in Schweiger 1984, p. 18; Sekler 1973, p. 141.
13 For Popischil, *Kunst und Kunsthandwerk*, vol. 4, 1901, p. 3; for Moser's room setting, *Ver Sacrum*, vol. 5, 1902, p. 323; for Hoffmann's furniture, Sekler 1985, pp. 39-40; for the Wiener Werkstätte, *Deutsche Kunst und Dekoration*, vol. 16, 1905, p. 524, and Schweiger 1984, p. 29. Light fittings by Hugo Ludwig (*Kunst und Kunsthandwerk*, vol. 7, 1904, p. 24) and Hoffmann (*Das Interieur*, vol. 4, 1903,

pp. 137, 140 and 164) may have been modelled on Mackintosh's.
14 Schweiger 1984, pp. 246-47, n. 72; Sekler 1973, p. 136.
15 Sekler 1973, p. 136; Kossatz 1971, p. 16.
16 Sekler 1985, p. 508, n. 37.
17 Howarth 1990, p. 185.
18 Robertson 1990, p. 220.
19 ibid., p. 223.
20 Muthesius 1902, p. 206.
21 ibid., p. 194.
22 p. 204.
23 p. 217.
24 p. 215.
25 Brett 1992, p. 65.
26 1902, vol. 26, p. 94.
27 Quoted in Pevsner 1968, p. 161.
28 Vol. 5, 1902, pp. 598-99.
29 Quoted in Billcliffe 1986, p. 125.
30 Quoted in Howarth 1990, p. 156.
31 Blackie 1968, p. 7.
32 ibid., p. 8.
33 ibid.
34 See the Reports on Buildings in the archives of the Dean of Guild (SRA). The application for work on 213-217 Sauchiehall Street passed the Court on 12 March 1903.
35 Viennese squares: compare Hoffmann's decorations for the fourteenth Secession exhibition (*Deutsche Kunst und Dekoration*, vol. 10, 1902, pp. 483-89); Carl Witzmann's Villa Bergmann in Pressbaum, which also has chequerboards like those at The Hill House (*Das Interieur*, vol. 3, 1902, p. 137); and the 'Austrian villa' by L. Baumann exhibited at Turin in 1902 (*Kunst und Kunsthandwerk*, vol. 5, 1902, pp. 406-7, 411-16).
36 Drawings in the archives of the Dean of Guild (SRA) suggest that the back extension existed before 1903 and was not added by Mackintosh.
37 Kinchin 1991, p. 110.
38 *Glasgow Evening News*, 29 Oct. 1903, p. 7; *Bailie*, 4 Nov. 1903, p. 6.
39 Viennese triangles: compare Moser's poster for the thirteenth Secession exhibition (*Ver Sacrum*, vol. 5, 1902, p. [94]) and the frieze at that exhibition (ibid., pp. 95 and 106); wall decorations in the Café Ronacher by Richard Seifert (*Das Interieur*, vol. 3, 1902, pp. 54-55); and Klimt's Beethoven frieze (*Ver Sacrum*, vol. 5, 1902, p. 172). See also Alofsin 1993, pp. 189-93.
40 Burkhauser 1990, p. 121.
41 For Witzmann's exhibit see *Deutsche Kunst und Dekoration*, vol. 11, 1902-3, pp. 78-79.

42 See Hoffmann's furniture illustrated in *Das Interieur*, vol. 4, 1903, p. 2, and Moser's Purkersdorf armchair of 1902, in Kirk Varnedoe, *Wien 1900: Kunst Architektur & Design*, Cologne 1987, p. 83.
43 Margaret Macdonald Mackintosh to Hermann Muthesius, Christmas 1904 (HAG).
44 Vol. 8, 1905, p. 198.
45 Alison 1973, p. 23. See also Philip Morton Shand's entry for Mackintosh in J. R. H. Weaver (ed.), *The Dictionary of National Biography 1922-1930*, London 1937: 'Mackintosh's influence on Continental design during the pre-War decade can hardly be exaggerated.'
46 Nuttgens 1988, p. 98.
47 Howarth 1990, p. 38.
48 ibid., p. 169.
49 Light fittings: *Deutsche Kunst und Dekoration*, vol. 11, 1902-3, p. 291; Posen: *Berliner Architektur*, vol. 7, 1904-5, p. 26; Grenander's pupils: *Moderne Bauformen*, vol. 6, 1907, pp. 316-28.
50 For Behrens, Alan Windsor, *Peter Behrens: Architect and Designer*, London 1981, pp. 56-57. For Muthesius, 'Mein Haus in Nikolassee', *Deutsche Kunst und Dekoration*, vol. 23, 1908-9, pp. 1-21.
51 p. 186.
52 Neat 1994, p. 24.
53 Elemér Czakó, 'A bécsi Szecesszió kiállítása', *Magyar Iparművészet*, vol. 4, 1901, pp. 40-41, and 'A torinoi kiállítás, *Magyar Iparművészet*, vol. 5, 1902, pp. 146, 154-55.
54 Vol. 21, 1907, p. 163.
55 The Art-Lover's House was illustrated in *American Architect and Building News*, 24 Sept. 1904. For Ellis's debts to Mackintosh see Wendy Kaplan (ed.), '*The Art that is Life*', Boston 1987, pp. 93-94, 114, and A. Patricia Bartinique, *Gustav Stickley: His Craft*, Parsippany, N. J., 1992, p. 48. Limbert's *Catalogue 100*, apparently dated Fall 1905, shows that he had seen Fernando Agnoletti's articles on the Willow Tea Rooms (*Dekorative Kunst*, vol. 13, 1905, pp. 257-75) and The Hill House (*Deutsche Kunst und Dekoration*, vol. 15, 1905, pp.

337-68); see also Kaplan, pp. 165-66. The decorative use of squares in the work of Karl Kipp and Dard Hunter of the Roycroft Community is probably best explained by their interest in Viennese work. The work of Greene and Greene in California has something of the spirit of Mackintosh's work, which Charles Sumner Greene probably saw when he visited Glasgow in 1901 and 1909; but there is no specific evidence of Mackintosh's influence on Greene and Greene, and similar details are probably due to a common inspiration from Japan.
56 Alofsin 1993, pp. 20 and 328-29.
57 Nuttgens 1988, p. 6.
58 Letter in the possession of the Charles Rennie Mackintosh Society.
59 Minutes of the School Board of Glasgow, 30 and 31 Oct. 1905 (SRA).
60 ibid., 14 Nov. 1905; and Gavin Stamp, 'School Lessons', *Architects' Journal*, 6 Apr. 1988, p. 50.
61 Vol. 39, 1906, p. 36.
62 Mackintosh to Anna Muthesius, 27 Mar. 1903 (HAG).

Chapter Four (pp. 141-62)
1 Howarth 1990, p. 111.
2 Correspondence relating to the extension of the School (GSA).
3 Mackintosh to Newbery, 4 June 1907. Correspondence relating to the extension of the School (GSA).
4 *Glasgow Herald*, 16 Dec. 1909, p. 5.
5 Macleod 1983, p. 134.
6 Howarth 1990, pp. 194-95.
7 Pevsner 1968, p. 174.
8 For lozenges, see Otto Prutscher's design for a crypt in Alofsin 1993, p. 195; and Marcel Kammerer's interior at the 1908 Kunstschau in *Moderne Bauformen*, vol. 7, 1908, p. 394.
9 Quoted in Stamp 1992, p. 24.
10 Bedford and Davies 1973, p. 285.
11 Blackie 1968, p. 8.
12 Margaret to Anna Geddes, 14 Jan. 1915 (Geddes Papers, National Library of Scotland, Edinburgh).
13 Howarth 1990, pp. 195-96.

Chapter Five (pp. 163-86)
1 Letter of June (?) 1915 (HAG).
2 Letter of 14 Jan. 1915 (Geddes Papers, National Library of Scotland, Edinburgh).
3 Moffat 1989, p. 80.
4 ibid., p. 79.
5 Margaret to William Davidson, 2 Feb. 1919 (HAG).
6 For Moser, see above, Chapter Three, n. 39; for Urban, Charles Holme (ed.), *The Art-Revival in Austria*, London 1906, C57-61 and 64.
7 (HAG).
8 ibid.
9 Letter of 12 Aug. 1919 (HAG).
10 For Hoffmann and stripes see *Dekorative Kunst*, vol. 4, 1899, p. 38, and *Das Interieur*, vol. 4, 1903, pp. 2, 148. For Ofner and Prutscher see Charles Holme (ed.), *The Art-Revival in Austria*, 1906, C36, 53-54.
11 Howarth 1990, p. 203.
12 Sale particulars of 8 July 1914 (Chelsea Public Library, London).
13 Diary, 17 June 1920 (HAG).

Chapter Six (pp. 187-93)
1 Moffat 1989, p. 110.
2 ibid., p. 113.
3 1924, p. 129.
4 Moffat 1989, p. 156.
5 Letter of 10 Jan. 1933 (HAG).

Chapter Seven (pp. 194-206)
1 Vol. 10, 1933, p. 98.
2 Quoted in Stamp 1992, p. 29.
3 Shand to Macdonald Smith & Co. 20 Mar. 1933 (HAG).
4 *Architectural Review*, vol. 77, 1935, pp. 23-26.
5 Milan 1950, pp. 31-32, trans. in Pevsner 1968, p. 162.
6 Howarth 1990, pp. 75, 138.
7 ibid., p. 89.
8 McLaren Young 1968, p. 5.
9 Macleod 1968, p. 9.
10 Brett 1992, p. 76.
11 Sunday *New York Times*, 24 Nov. 1974.

Bibliography

Alison, Filippo, *Charles Rennie Mackintosh as a Designer of Chairs*, 2nd edn, London 1978
Alofsin, Anthony, *Frank Lloyd Wright: The Lost Years, 1910– 1922: A Study of Influence*, Chicago 1993

Barnes, H. Jefferson, *Charles Rennie Mackintosh and Glasgow School of Art: 1: The Architecture, Exteriors and Interiors*, 3rd edn, Glasgow 1988
—, *Charles Rennie Mackintosh and Glasgow School of Art: Furniture in the*

School Collection, 2nd edn, Glasgow 1978
—, *Charles Rennie Mackintosh and Glasgow School of Art: 3: Ironwork and Metalwork at Glasgow School of Art*, 2nd edn, Glasgow 1978

Bedford, June, and Ivor Davies, 'Remembering Charles Rennie Mackintosh: A Recorded Interview with Mrs. Mary Sturrock', *Connoisseur*, vol. 183, 1973, pp. 280-88

Billcliffe, Roger, 'J. H. MacNair in Glasgow and Liverpool' in Walker Art Gallery, Liverpool, *Annual Report & Bulletin*, vol. 1, 1970-71, pp. 48-74

—, *Architectural Sketches and Flower Drawings by Charles Rennie Mackintosh*, London and New York 1977

—, *Mackintosh Watercolours*, London 1978

—, *Mackintosh Furniture*, Cambridge 1984

—, *Charles Rennie Mackintosh: The Complete Furniture, Furniture Drawings & Interior Designs*, London and New York 1979, 3rd edn, London 1986

—, *Mackintosh Textile Designs*, 2nd edn, San Francisco 1993

Billcliffe, Roger, and Peter Vergo, 'Charles Rennie Mackintosh and the Austrian Art Revival', *Burlington Magazine*, vol. 119, 1977, pp. 739-46

Bird, Elizabeth, 'Ghouls and Gas Pipes: Public Reaction to the early work of The Four', *Scottish Art Review*, vol. 14, 1975, pp. 13-16

Blackie, Walter, 'Memories of Charles Rennie Mackintosh', *Scottish Art Review*, vol. 11, 1968, pp. 6-11

Brett, David, 'The Eroticization of Domestic Space: A Mirror by C. R. Mackintosh', *Journal of Decorative and Propaganda Arts*, vol. 10, 1988, pp. 6-13

—, *C. R. Mackintosh: The Poetics of Workmanship*, London and Cambridge, Mass., 1992

Buchanan, William (ed.), *Mackintosh's Masterwork: The Glasgow School of Art*, Glasgow and San Francisco 1989

Burkhauser, Jude (ed.), *'Glasgow Girls': Women in Art and Design 1880-1928*, Edinburgh 1990

Christie's (London), *The Dr. Thomas Howarth Collection*, sale cat., 17 Feb. 1994

Cooper, Jackie (ed.), *Mackintosh Architecture: The Complete Buildings and Selected Projects*, London and New York 1978, 2nd edn, London 1980

Eadie, William, *Movements of Modernity: The Case of Glasgow and Art Nouveau*, London 1990

Edinburgh Festival Society and Scottish Arts Council (text by Andrew McLaren Young), *Charles Rennie*

Mackintosh (1868-1928): Architecture, Design and Painting, exhibition cat., 1968,

Glasgow Museums and Art Galleries, *The Glasgow Style 1890-1920*, exhibition cat., 1984

Gomme, Andor, and David Walker, *Architecture of Glasgow*, 2nd edn, London and Glasgow 1987

Helland, Janice, 'Frances Macdonald: The Self as Fin-de-Siècle Woman', *Woman's Art Journal*, Spring-Summer 1993, pp. 15-22

—, 'The Critics and the Arts and Crafts: The Instance of Margaret Macdonald and Charles Rennie Mackintosh', *Art History*, vol. 17, 1994, pp. 209-27

Howarth, Thomas, *Charles Rennie Mackintosh and the Modern Movement*, London 1952; 3rd edn, London 1990

Hunterian Art Gallery, University of Glasgow (text by Pamela Reekie), *Margaret Macdonald Mackintosh*, exhibition cat., 1983

— (text by Pamela Robertson), *Mackintosh Flower Drawings*, exhibition cat., 1988

— (text by Pamela Robertson), *The Estate and Collection of Works by Charles Rennie Mackintosh at the Hunterian Art Gallery, University of Glasgow*, Glasgow 1991

— (text by Janet Bassett-Lowke and Alan Crawford), *C. R. Mackintosh: The Chelsea Years 1915-1923*, exhibition cat., 1994

Jones, Anthony, *Charles Rennie Mackintosh*, London and Edison, N. J., 1990

Kinchin, Perilla, *Tea and Taste: The Glasgow Tea Rooms 1875—1975*, Wendlebury, Oxon, 1991

Kossatz, Horst-Herbert, 'The Vienna Secession and its early relations with Great Britain', *Studio International*, vol. 181, 1971, pp. 9-19

Macaulay, James, *Charles Rennie Mackintosh: Glasgow School of Art*, London 1993

—, *Charles Rennie Mackintosh: Hill House*, London 1994

Macleod, Robert, *Charles Rennie Mackintosh: Architect and Artist*, Feltham, Mx 1968; 2nd edn, London 1983

Moffat, Alistair and Colin Baxter, *Remembering Charles Rennie Mackintosh: An Illustrated Biography*, Lanark 1989

Moon, Karen, *George Walton, Designer and Architect*, Oxford 1993

Muthesius, Hermann, 'Die Glasgower Kunstbewegung: Charles R. Mackintosh und Margaret Macdonald-Mackintosh', *Dekorative*

Kunst, vol. 9, 1902, pp. 193-221

—, *The English House*, London 1979, an abridgement of the 2nd edn of Muthesius's *Das englische Haus* (Berlin 1904-5; 2nd edn., Berlin 1908-11), ed. by Dennis Sharp and trans. by Janet Seligmann

Neat, Timothy, *Part Seen, Part Imagined: Meaning and Symbolism in the Work of Charles Rennie Mackintosh and Margaret Macdonald*, Edinburgh 1994

Nuttgens, Patrick (ed.), *Mackintosh & his Contemporaries in Europe and America*, London 1988

Pevsner, Nikolaus, 'Charles Rennie Mackintosh' in Pevsner, *Studies in Art, Architecture and Design: Volume Two: Victorian and After*, London and New York 1968, pp. 152-75, a revision and translation of *Charles R. Mackintosh* (Milan 1950)

Posener, Julius, 'Hermann Muthesius and English Domestic Architecture', *Architectural Association Quarterly*, vol. 12, 1980, no. 2, pp. 54-61.

Robertson, Pamela (ed.), *Charles Rennie Mackintosh: The Architectural Papers*, Wendlebury, Oxon, and Cambridge, Mass., 1990

Savage, Peter, *Lorimer and the Edinburgh Craft Designers*, Edinburgh 1980

Schweiger, Werner J., *Wiener Werkstaette: Design in Vienna 1903-1932*, London 1984/New York 1990

Sekler, Eduard, 'Mackintosh and Vienna' in Nikolaus Pevsner and J. M. Richards (eds), *The Anti-Rationalists*, London and New York 1973, pp. 136-42

—, *Josef Hoffmann: The Architectural Work*, Princeton, N. J., 1985

Stamp, Gavin, 'Mackintosh, Burnet and Modernity' in John Lowrey (ed.), *Architectural Heritage III: The Age of Mackintosh*, Edinburgh 1992, pp. 8-31

Summerson, John, 'The British Contemporaries of Frank Lloyd Wright' in Summerson, *The Unromantic Castle*, London 1990, pp. 237-44

Vergo, Peter, *Art in Vienna, 1898-1918*, London 1975, /Ithaca, N. Y., 1981

Walker, David, 'The Early Work of Charles Rennie Mackintosh', in Nikolaus Pevsner and J. M. Richards (eds), *The Anti-Rationalists*, London and New York 1973, pp. 116-35

—, 'Scotland and Paris 1874-1887' in John Frew and David Jones (eds), *Scotland and Europe: Architecture and Design 1850-1940*, St Andrews 1991, pp. 15-40

Williamson, Elizabeth, Anne Riches and Malcolm Higgs, *The Buildings of Scotland: Glasgow*, Edinburgh 1990

Buildings and Interiors by Mackintosh

This is a summary list of buildings, monuments, interiors, exhibition room settings, and some furniture schemes designed by Mackintosh, sometimes in collaboration with his wife, Margaret Macdonald Mackintosh. For more information, readers should consult Walker 1973, Cooper 1980, Billcliffe 1986 and Howarth 1990 (see the Bibliography).

The list is not as complete as one would wish. For instance, on 19 November 1902 Mackintosh told Hermann Muthesius that he had designed eight competition entries in the previous six months; none of these can be identified from his surviving drawings. It is also crude: much of Mackintosh's architectural work was done within the office of Honeyman and Keppie, later Honeyman Keppie and Mackintosh. In many cases we may know from documentary evidence that Mackintosh was involved in a building, but we cannot tell how far. Where there is some doubt about the fact or extent of Mackintosh's involvement, the entry is marked by an asterisk (*).

The list includes unexecuted as well as executed work, but it does not include unidentified and undated designs which were not developed beyond a few sketches.

The works are listed, so far as possible, in the order in which they were designed. In the case of executed work, the dates cover the period of design and execution.

The names of current administrative areas are given in brackets.

Many of the principal Mackintosh buildings are open to the public, and they are marked in this list with a #. For details of opening times, please refer to the Charles Rennie Mackintosh Society, Queen's Cross, 870 Garscube Road, Glasgow G20 7EL, tel. 041–946–6600.

1888 A mountain chapel. Design entered in the National Competition.
1888 A town house in a terrace. Student design awarded a prize by the Glasgow Institute of the Fine Arts.
1888 Gravestone for Chief Constable Andrew McCall, the Necropolis, Glasgow 4.
*1888–89 Wylie Hill's store, 20–24 Buchanan Street, Glasgow 1. Designed by John Hutchison; the decorative sculpture may have been designed by Mackintosh.

1889 A Presbyterian church. Competition design.
1890 A science and art museum. Design entered in the National Competition.
1890 A public hall. Design entered in competition for the Alexander Thomson Travelling Studentship.
1890 Nos. 120–122 (now 140–142) Balgrayhill Road, Springburn, Glasgow 21. A pair of semi-detached houses for William Hamilton, Mackintosh's uncle.
1890 Workmen's dwellings, High Street and Rottenrow, Glasgow 4. Competition design for the City of Glasgow Improvement Trust.
1891 A chapter house. Design entered in the RIBA Soane Medallion Competition.
*1891–93 Canal Boatmen's Institute, Dobbies Loan and Port Dundas Road, Glasgow 4. For the Canal Boatmen's Friend Society of Scotland. Demolished.
*1891–92 Glasgow Art Galleries, Kelvingrove Park, Glasgow 3. Competition design for the Association for the Promotion of Art and Music.
*1892 Manchester Municipal Technical Schools, London Road and Oxford Road, Manchester. Competition design.
1892 A railway terminus. Design entered in the RIBA Soane Medallion Competition.
#*1892–93 (probable date) Alterations and additions, Craigie Hall, 6 Rowan Road, Glasgow 41. For Thomas Mason. Mackintosh's hand is most obvious in the decorative detail of the library.
*1892–93 Alterations and additions, the Glasgow Art Club, 187–191 Bath Street, Glasgow 2. For the Glasgow Art Club.
1893–95 Premises for The Glasgow Herald, 68–76 Mitchell Street, Glasgow 1. For George Outram and Company.
*1894–95 40 Sinclair Street, Helensburgh, Dunbartonshire (Strathclyde). For Helensburgh and Gareloch Conservative Club.
*1894–95 Anatomy School, Queen Margaret's College (now Broadcasting House), Queen Margaret Drive, Glasgow 12. For the University Court, University of Glasgow.
*1894 Premises for the Royal Insurance Company, Buchanan Street, Glasgow 1. Competition design.

1894–95 Design for a library in a Glasgow house.
*1895–97 Martyrs' Public School, 11 Parson Street, Glasgow 4. For the School Board of Glasgow.
*1895 Alterations, Lennox Castle Inn, Lennoxtown, Stirlingshire (Strathclyde).
*1895 St Paul's Church Mission Hall, 16–22 Shuttle Street and 33–39 College Lane, Glasgow 1.
*1896–97 Premises for The Glasgow Herald: rebuilding the central portion between the Mitchell Street building and the original premises at 65 Buchanan Street, Glasgow 1. For George Outram and Company.
#1896–99 Glasgow School of Art, 167 Renfrew Street, Glasgow 3 (first phase). For the Governors of Glasgow School of Art.
1896–97 Decorations, Miss Cranston's Tea Rooms, 91–93 Buchanan Street, Glasgow 1. For Miss Catherine Cranston. Destroyed.
#1897–99 Queen's Cross Church, 870 Garscube Road, Glasgow 20. For the Deacon's Court of Free St Matthew's Church.
#1897 Interior of the music room, Craigie Hall, 6 Rowan Road, Glasgow 41. For Thomas Mason.
1898 Gravestone for James Reid in the cemetery, Kilmacolm, Renfrewshire (Strathclyde).
1898 Buildings for Glasgow International Exhibition, Kelvingrove Park, Glasgow 3. Competition designs for Glasgow International Exhibition Association.
1898 Premises for the National Bank of Scotland, St Vincent and Buchanan Streets, Glasgow 1. Competition design.
1898 (probable date) Interior of a bedroom, Westdel, 2 Queen's Place, Downanhill, Glasgow 12. For Robert Maclehose.
1898 (probable date) Interior of a dining room, Nymphenburgerstrasse 86, Munich, Germany. For Hugo Bruckmann.
1898–99 Furniture for Miss Cranston's Tea Rooms, 114 Argyle Street, Glasgow 3. For Miss Catherine Cranston.
*1898–99 Alterations, additions and interiors, 233 St Vincent Street, Glasgow 2. For H. L. Anderson and Co.
*1898–99 Redlands (now Beauly), Hazelwood Road, Bridge of Weir, Renfrewshire (Strathclyde).

1898–99 Ruchill Street Free Church Halls, 24 Ruchill Street, Glasgow 20. For the Trustees for the Congregation of Westbourne Free Church.

1899 Pulpit and choir stalls, Gourock Parish Church, Renfrewshire (Strathclyde).

*__1899–1901__ Pettigrew and Stephens department store, 185–193 Sauchiehall Street, Glasgow 3. For Andrew H. Pettigrew. Demolished. The cupola, attributed to Mackintosh on stylistic grounds, is now in the Hunterian Art Gallery.

1899–1900 Interiors, 120 Mains Street (now Blythswood Street), Glasgow 2. For himself and Margaret Macdonald. The interior was partly dismantled when the Mackintoshes moved to 6 Florentine Terrace.

1900 (probable date) Interior of the drawing room, Dunglass Castle, Bowling, Dunbartonshire (Strathclyde). For Charles Macdonald. Destroyed.

1900 Interiors of the ladies' lunch room, billiard room, smoking room and rear tea room, Miss Cranston's Tea Rooms, 205–215 Ingram Street, Glasgow 1. For Miss Catherine Cranston. Removed; now in the care of Glasgow Museums.

1900–1901, 1903–4 Printing offices for *The Daily Record*, 20–28 Renfield Lane, Glasgow 2. For *The Daily Record* Newspaper (Limited), Glasgow.

1900–1901 Windyhill, Houston Street, Kilmacolm, Renfrewshire (Strathclyde). For William Davidson.

1900 Room setting, eighth exhibition of the Vienna Secession.

c. **1900** Design for a country mansion.

1900–1901 A House for an Art Lover. Competition design for Alexander Koch.

1901 Exhibition stands, Glasgow International Exhibition.

1901 Alterations and additions, 29 Hamilton Drive, Glasgow 12. For Alex Frew.

c. **1901** Decorations, St Serf's Church, Dysart, Fife.

c. **1901** Design for a golf clubhouse.

c. **1901** An artist's house in the country. Speculative design.

c. **1901** An artist's house in the town. Speculative design.

1901–2 Fitted furniture, 3 Lilybank Terrace, Glasgow 12. For R. Wylie Hill.

1901–2 Interiors of the hall and drawing room, 14 (now 34) Kingsborough Gardens, Glasgow 12. For Mrs Robert J. Rowat.

1901–2 Gate lodge, Auchenbothie, Port Glasgow Road, Kilmacolm,

Renfrewshire (Strathclyde). For Hugh Brown Collins.

1901–2 Anglican Cathedral, St James's Mount, Liverpool. Competition design.

#__1902–4__ The Hill House, Upper Colquhoun Street, Helensburgh, Dunbartonshire (Strathclyde). For Walter W. Blackie.

1902 Scottish section, International Exhibition of Modern Decorative Art, Turin.

1902–3, 1906–8 Interior, music salon, Carl-Ludwigstrasse 45 (now Weimarstrasse 59), Vienna. For Fritz Wärndorfer. Destroyed.

1902 A house at Kilmacolm, Renfrewshire (Strathclyde). Possibly not executed.

1902–3 Room setting at the exhibition 'Architecture and Artistic Craft of the New Style', Moscow.

#__1903__ Alterations to 213 and 217 Sauchiehall Street, Glasgow 3. No. 213 for Miss Jessie Henderson, 217 for Miss Catherine Cranston (the Willow Tea Rooms). Today, 217 Sauchiehall Street is partly a survival and partly a reconstruction of the 1903 building.

1903–6 Scotland Street School, 255 Scotland Street, Glasgow 5. For the School Board of Glasgow.

1903–4 Interior of a bedroom for an exhibition organized by the Dresdener Werkstätte für Handwerkskunst, Dresden.

1904 Pulpit, communion table and chairs, organ screen and choir stalls, Holy Trinity church, Bridge of Allan, Stirlingshire (Central Region).

1904–5 Interiors, Hous'hill, Nitshill, Glasgow. For Major John Cochrane and Miss Catherine Cranston. Demolished.

1904–5 New porch, Arddarroch, near Loch Goil, Whistlefield, Dunbartonshire (Strathclyde). For Mr Brooman White.

1904–5 Shop at 233 Sauchiehall Street, Glasgow 3. For Henry and Carruthers, drapers.

1905 Dining-room interior for an exhibition in the showrooms of A. S. Ball, Berlin.

1905 Wellesley Tea Rooms, 145 Sauchiehall Street, Glasgow 3. For the Trustees of the late Dr Walker. Only the plan was by Mackintosh.

1905 Gravestone for the Rev. Alexander Orrock Johnston, Wemyss Castle, Fife.

1905–6 Pulpit, organ case, font, light fittings and decorations, Abbey Close United Free Church, Paisley, Renfrewshire (Strathclyde). Demolished.

1905–8 Auchinibert, Killearn, Stirlingshire (Central Region). For Francis J. Shand.

1906 Interior, the Dutch Kitchen, Miss Cranston's Tea Rooms, 114 Argyle Street, Glasgow 3. For Miss Catherine Cranston.

1906 Alterations and interior decorations, 6 Florentine Terrace (later 78 Southpark Avenue), Glasgow 12. For himself and Margaret Macdonald. The house itself was demolished in 1963, but the interiors have been reconstructed as The Mackintosh House, part of the Hunterian Art Gallery of the University of Glasgow.

1906 Alterations, 9 Grosvenor Terrace, Glasgow 12. For Sigurd Röed. Not executed.

1906 Exhibition stand for Wilkinson Heywood and Clark Ltd.

1906 Balgray Cottage, Cloak, Kilmacolm, Renfrewshire (Strathclyde). For Hugh Brown Collins.

#__1906__ Interior of the board room, Glasgow School of Art, 167 Renfrew Street, Glasgow 3. For the Governors of Glasgow School of Art.

#__1907–9__ Glasgow School of Art, 167 Renfrew Street, Glasgow 3 (second phase). For the Governors of Glasgow School of Art.

1907 Interior of the Oak Room, Miss Cranston's Tea Rooms, 205–217 Ingram Street, Glasgow 1. For Miss Catherine Cranston. Removed; now in the care of Glasgow Museums.

1907–8 Additions, The Moss, Dumgoyne, Killearn, Stirlingshire (Central Region). For Sir Archibald Lawrie.

1908 Mossyde, Cloak, Kilmacolm, Renfrewshire (Strathclyde). For Hugh Brown Collins. This is an extension of Balgray Cottage, (see above, 1906).

1908 New entrance and interiors, 5 Blythswood Square, Glasgow 2. For the Lady Artists' Club.

1909 Interior of the Card Room, Hous'hill, Nitshill, Glasgow. For Major John Cochrane and Miss Catherine Cranston. Demolished.

1909–10 Interiors of the Oval Room and the ladies' rest room, Miss Cranston's Tea Rooms, 205–217 Ingram Street, Glasgow 1. For Miss Catherine Cranston. Removed; now in the care of Glasgow Museums.

1911 Interior of the White Cockade Tea Room, Scottish National Exhibition, Kelvingrove Park, Glasgow 3. For Miss Catherine Cranston. Demolished.

1911 Interior of the Chinese Room, Miss Cranston's Tea Rooms, 205–217

Ingram Street, Glasgow 1. For Miss Catherine Cranston. Removed; now in the care of Glasgow Museums.
1911 Gravestone for Talwin Morris, public cemetery, Dumbarton, Dunbartonshire (Strathclyde).
1911–12 Interior of the Cloister Room, Miss Cranston's Tea Rooms, 205–217 Ingram Street, Glasgow 1. For Miss Catherine Cranston. Removed; now in the care of Glasgow Museums.
1911–13 Alterations and additions to Auchenbothie Mains, Port Glasgow Road, Kilmacolm, Renfrewshire (Strathclyde). For Hugh Brown Collins.
1912 Interior of a ladies' hairdressing salon, 80 Union Street, Glasgow 1. For Mr Ritchie. Demolished.
1913 Additions to Mossyde, Cloak, Kilmacolm, Renfrewshire (Strathclyde). For Hugh Brown Collins.
c. **1915** Design for a shop- and office-block in an arcaded street. Speculative design, possibly for Patrick Geddes.
c. **1915** Design for a warehouse-block in an arcaded street. Speculative design, possibly for Patrick Geddes.

c. **1915** A memorial fountain in a public place. Speculative design, probably for Patrick Geddes.
c. **1915** Designs for lamp standards. Speculative designs, probably for Patrick Geddes.
c. **1915** A war memorial in a public place. Speculative design, probably for Patrick Geddes.
1916–17 Alterations and additions, 78 Derngate, Northampton. For Wenman J. Bassett-Lowke.
1916–17 Interior of the Dug-Out, Willow Tea Rooms, 217 Sauchiehall Street, Glasgow 3. For Miss Catherine Cranston. Demolished.
1917 Interior of a bedroom, Fairlawn, Weston Road, Bath, Somerset (Avon). For Sidney Horstmann.
1918–19 Alterations, additions and interior of the dining room, Candida Cottage, Roade, Northamptonshire. For Wenman J. Bassett-Lowke.
1919 Interior of the dining room, 5 The Drive, Northampton. For J. M. Jones.
1919 Alterations and additions, Little Hedgecourt, near East Grinstead, West Sussex. For E. O. Hoppé.
1919 Interior of the guest bedroom, 78 Derngate, Northampton. For

Wenman J. Bassett-Lowke.
1920–21 Studio-house, 49 Glebe Place, Chelsea, London. For Harold Squire.
1920 Studio-house, 48 Glebe Place, Chelsea, London. For Arthur Cadogan Blunt. Not executed.
1920 Studios, 50 Glebe Place, Chelsea, London. For Francis Derwent Wood. Not executed.
1920 Alterations, the Mystery House, Upper Cheyne Row, Chelsea, London. 1920. For the Arts League of Service. Not executed.
1920 A block of studios and studio-flats on the site of Cheyne House, Upper Cheyne Row, Chelsea, London. For the Arts League of Service. Not executed.
1920 A theatre, Chelsea, London. For Margaret Morris. Not executed.
1920–21 Alterations and additions to Leigh Farm Cottages, Ansty, West Sussex. For Miss Florence Brooks.
1920 or later A block of studios and possibly studio-flats, 48 Glebe Place, Chelsea, London. For the Arts League of Service. Not executed.
1921 Redecoration of the hall, 78 Derngate, Northampton. For Wenman J. Bassett-Lowke.

Public Collections containing Work by Mackintosh

A good deal of Mackintosh's work in the decorative arts is in private hands. But an even larger amount is in public collections, and the most important of those are listed here.

AUSTRALIA Canberra The National Gallery of Australia

AUSTRIA Vienna Österreichisches Museum für angewandte Kunst

CANADA Ottawa The National Gallery; **Toronto**: Royal Ontario Museum

FRANCE Paris Musée d'Orsay

GERMANY Darmstadt Museum Künstlerkolonie; **Hamburg** Museum für Kunst und Gewerbe

GREAT BRITAIN The largest collection of Mackintosh's work is in **Glasgow**, in the University of

Glasgow's Hunterian Art Gallery, to which the collection of drawings, watercolours and archival material which constituted Mackintosh's Estate passed in 1947. Furniture formerly in the Mackintoshes' possession was given by the Davidson family in 1946. The Gallery also includes the reconstructed interiors of 6 Florentine Terrace, known as The Mackintosh House. The second largest collection is in the possession of Glasgow School of Art, and includes furniture from Windyhill and from several of Miss Cranston's Tea Rooms. Glasgow Museum and Art Gallery has Mackintosh material, including the interiors from Miss Cranston's Tea Rooms in Ingram Street, parts of which are currently being reconstructed. Miscellaneous drawings by Mackintosh are in the possession of Dumbarton Planning Department, the National Trust for Scotland, Strathclyde Regional Archives and the archives of the University of Strathclyde.

Other public collections containing work by Mackintosh include **Brighton** Brighton Museum and Art Gallery; **Edinburgh** Scottish National Gallery of Modern Art, The National Museums of Scotland; **London** British Museum, Royal Institute of British Architects Drawings Collection, Tate Gallery, Victoria and Albert Museum; **Northampton** Northampton Museum; **Sheffield** Graves Art Gallery

IRELAND Dublin National Library of Ireland

UNITED STATES Chicago Art Institute of Chicago; **Detroit** Detroit Institute of Arts; **Los Angeles** Los Angeles County Museum of Art; **Miami** Wolfsonian Foundation; **New York** Metropolitan Museum of Art, Museum of Modern Art; **Richmond**, Virginia Museum of Fine Arts

Index